ADHD in Marriage

Real and Proven Ways to Keep Your Marriage Thriving Despite the Chaos, Overcome Denial, and Insulate Your Relationship from Stress – Includes Q&A

Dr. Melody Dawson

Table of Contents

Introduction

Nothing hurts as much as the agony of a bad relationship. Can we fix it or should we throw it out? If someone wants to leave their marriage, they might have a hard time. They will think about all the consequences to make sure they are ready. During this time, they will hurt inside from what the other person is doing to them. They might have guilt because they are hurting their spouse too. Sometimes, we are sure of everything while at other times, we are lost. When children are involved, the intensity of the conflict is multiplied by the factor of a million! When ADHD enters the scene, it adds a whole new level of difficulty and anguish.

ADHD is currently considered to be one of the most common disorders affecting the brain, with a worldwide prevalence of about 5% among children and adolescents. Although for most adults in 60 to 70% of cases, the ADHD persists into adulthood, either as a residual condition or a full clinical disorder, we need to be aware and sympathetic to it when working with the afflicted.

A Quick Overview of ADHD

Since school has started, parents and teachers will be paying close attention to their children's academic achievement and classroom behavior. Some people first notice a youngster having difficulties paying attention, sitting still, remembering, or following the rules at school. These youngsters are frequently referred for psychological testing to rule out ADHD, which is a combination of numerous problems. When the primary concern is attention, it is commonly referred to as ADD (attention deficit disorder).

Daniel Amen, a psychiatrist and researcher who uses SPECT (Single-Proton Emission Computerized Tomography) imaging of the brain to examine how its various systems work defines six forms of ADHD. According to his findings from these brain scans, blood flow to the prefrontal cortex, the area responsible for decision-making, judgment, and processing consequences is diminished in most types of ADHD. Thus, ADHD is not a made-up diagnosis or a label applied to all misbehaving children: it is a real biological condition, as evidenced by brain scans.

One conclusion about ADHD appears to be obvious: the child tends to daydream or is easily distracted. They cannot sit still or follow directions. It can be one or more of these symptoms. Social and emotional consequences can substantially impact self-esteem and the capacity to relate well to others.

ADIID's Social and Emotional Consequences

As relational beings, each of us expects others in our world to love, accept, believe in, and even cherish us. We know that loving a child properly is crucial for the child's sense of self, whether we understand healthy human development through the eyes of modern psychological science or the eyes of our faith and understanding of morality. The perspective we take will lay the groundwork for feeling competent in the world and treating others with respect and dignity. Creating a healthy sense of self is essential for success in both work and relationships.

The issue is that children with ADHD, in any form, can be exceedingly difficult to handle. I can feel the frustration and stress of parents of ADHD children. If left undiagnosed and untreated, these children cannot recall what they have been told and may continually ping from one source of interest to the next flashy distraction. They CANNOT act like others with normal brain activity because there is no proper blood flow to the executive functioning center of the brain. As a result, it is highly difficult for teachers and other authority figures, including parents, to communicate effectively with these youngsters. They may need constant monitoring or supervision. They usually fall short of expectations. They frequently daydream, forget, or become sidetracked, resulting in rule violations. Soon, these children reach a key conclusion: "I am not like these other kids."

Aha. This epiphany may soon lead to further realizations such as "Adults do not like me... so I do not like them," or "Look at these normal youngsters, why cannot I be like them?" or "What is the matter with me?" The scene is set for more chronic behavioral disorders (Oppositional Defiant Disorder or Conduct Disorder). Many people with ADHD, particularly those who are quite bright, have some affection in their lives. They can demonstrate some skills and manage to muddle through school and into adulthood and a career. However, they treat the world as they believe they have been treated, projecting their frustration outward. When persons with ADHD go untreated, their frustration shift inward, leaving them vulnerable to depression and mood disorders, anxiety disorders, substance addiction, and other self-destructive behaviors.

Adult-Onset ADHD

It was once assumed that people grew out of their childhood attention deficit disorder (ADHD). We now know that this is not the case. Their instructors and parents tried to manage the anger, nagging, annoyance, yelling, shaming, comparing, and so on. Adults with undiagnosed or untreated ADHD may not have the boundless energy of a 7-year-old, and they might have learned how to avoid being singled out as they once were. But make no mistake: the blood flow/brain functioning issues do not simply disappear with age. Adults with untreated ADHD may struggle in college or find occupations that do not require a degree. Many people may move from one type of employment to the next. They find it challenging to work for bosses/supervisors/managers since those in positions of authority typically behave in the same nagging way. Adults with ADHD know how to have a good time and are fun to date (usually spontaneous, entertaining, and unpredictable), but these qualities may fade quickly with time.

ADHD in Relationships

It is very common for two people with ADHD to marry. Because each one know what it is like to be an "outsider," they may feel understood and accepted for the first time in their lives. This kinship experience may be fairly strong, so much so that because both may be impulsive, they may marry or live together and have children at a younger age than others. Again, because their brain's judgment area is damaged, they may have more children than their contemporaries. This frequently places these couples in what appears to be an impossible financial struggle to survive and provide for their families. Furthermore, because ADHD is typically passed down through families, at least one of the children may suffer from it. As a result, the couple is financially, emotionally, and relationally stressed.

Still, it is possible that a person with ADHD could meet someone who appears to be their total opposite: someone responsible who follows society's rules and laws and is attentive to details and deadlines. This is an example of how opposites attract: the ADHD spouse realizes that he (or she) can be loved by one of society's "normal." For someone with ADHD, this delivers a satisfying sense of control: "Finally, one of them likes me! Maybe I can be normal now." Moreover, for the non-ADHD spouse, living with someone with ADHD can feel exciting and liberating, especially for someone who has lived her (or his) entire life coloring within the lines. They both perceive the other as complementing them, filling the gap within.

However, the honeymoon period may be coming to an end as the couple's differences begin to weigh on each other. The partner who does not have ADHD starts to feel the pressure of juggling so many of life's continual demands. Perhaps she sees her spouse lose job after job or has disputes with boss one after another. She soon realizes that the financial stability of the household lies solely on her shoulders. (I am using her for the sake of convenience; ADHD can afflict both sexes.) Perhaps she sees her partner experiment with drugs and/or alcohol to dull the pain of life's setbacks. In the back of her mind, she begins to ponder what she once saw in him, resenting him for his "irresponsibility."

The spouse with ADHD, on the other hand, feels like a jerk who cannot live life like everyone else. He sees people working, making a living, and finding relative contentment all around; but just like at school, he is not one of them. Something is not right: it is either me...or them! He grows tired of his wife's continuous criticisms, and her dissatisfaction with him withers his soul.

Suppose the couple comes for couple's therapy. In that case, the non-ADHD spouse is frequently filled with disappointment, bitterness, and even hatred, while the ADHD spouse takes a defensive posture, wanting to be accepted as is. "You think you are so perfect!" is a common response to his spouse. However, underneath this time-tested defensive tactic, designed to shield him from the agony of relationship failure, comes a great deal of shame and self-loathing.

When One Spouse Suffers from ADHD

Couple's counseling, especially when one spouse has ADHD, can be a very rewarding experience. If there is love, there is hope. This does not mean that treatment will be simple; but with time, a couple may recognize ADHD as an issue and approach it as a team. Both the husband and wife's grief tend to depersonalize: instead of growing upset with the ADHD-affected spouse, they get irritated with ADHD (the disease). Instead of feeling flawed and useless, the ADHD- affected spouse now sees the illness as the problem, NOT HIMSELF! Yes, life would be better without ADHD, but millions of people in America alone suffer from it, and therapy is available. You can say, "I no longer have to experience life as I have up to this point, and the best is yet to come for me."

Please do not get me wrong: after years of being in an ADHD/non-ADHD sort of relationship, it can be tough to modify behavior patterns. Most likely, the non-ADHD spouse has been obligated to clean up everyone else's messes; she felt obliged to be the responsible one while others got to play. Perhaps she grew up with an emotionally needy mom (or both parents) and troubled siblings. Daring to let go of being the responsible one demands enormous bravery! "If I no longer must wear the burden of being the responsible one, what kind of person am I? That is the only way I know how to live in this world." It necessitates the co-creation of a new, more liberated self, requiring practice and time.

Meanwhile, the person with ADHD has grown accustomed to feeling incapable and sad, as if they were a rebel or an alien. They have prided themselves on marching to the beat of a different drummer. What happens when people learn that they can keep their individualism while also feeling welcome and productive members of the human race? It also takes a long time to imagine, practice, and appreciate!

When Both Husbands and Wives Have ADHD

When partners share this diagnosis, it can strengthen their relationship. "We knew it! We knew we were unique!" They initially seek treatment because their lives are in disaster mode. In addition, they may both use drink and/or drugs to assist them in numbing themselves from the pressures of the outside world. A failure to recognize and treat these conditions can lead to the emergence of brand-new problems. Therefore, the pair must accept the diagnosis and start therapy. If not, one will sabotage the other to protect their dynamic from changing. It might be frightening to imagine what the partnership might become: "Perhaps I will lose my spouse if he or she changes."

Today, many individuals start therapy without being diagnosed with ADHD, despite having significant attention and distractibility issues, a lack of follow-through, and/or impulsivity. Psychological testing and clinical contact with a therapist who is experienced with ADHD can aid in ruling in or out this diagnosis. When a diagnosis is made with ADHD, the child is referred to a physician, who may prescribe and monitor medications to improve brain function. Alternative treatments for ADHD include:

- Omega-3 oil and other food supplements
- Dietary modifications
- Neurofeedback (a computer-based program that rewards the brain for working in healthier ways)
- Adherence to a planning method

Planning methods could be computer-based or paper-based, in which one notices what is to be done and needed to check off when finished. It may be used alone or in conjunction with medication.

While many of the approaches listed above (and more are on the way) are beneficial, ACCEPTING the diagnosis may be the most crucial move a person with ADHD can take. For some, admitting the condition is extremely humiliating; it confirms that they are, in fact, imperfect. Others have difficulty trusting consultants (such as psychologists or physicians), which hinders their therapy. Others believe that admitting the truth about themselves signals defeat: "If I accept this, then they will win, and I can never give them the satisfaction!" What happens if the spouse is one of those voices? All that remains is a ruthless power battle, no fun!

ADHD certainly wreaks havoc on many marriages; it can be the boogeyman in the closet. However, like most monsters, it is revealed to be what it is once the light is turned on. Moreover, this monster can be defeated.

Chapter 1:
What is Attention Deficit Hyperactivity Disorder?

S ome doctors have recognized attention-deficit hyperactivity disorder—or as some people still call it, "ADD," short for attention-deficit disorder—since 1902. From 1902 to 1980, though, it was all about little boys who could not sit still and become quiet, and were continuously talking and driving everyone insane. However, it was simply a case of misbehavior.

The disorder's name has been altered several times. There were several formulas along the way. Nevertheless, it was all about behavioral issues. Since 1980, when they first modified the nomenclature of the condition to include the terms "attention deficit," we have discovered that this is significantly more of a problem with the brain's management system— its executive functions. We also discovered that many persons with ADHD have never experienced serious behavioral issues. Moreover, even for those who have, it is frequently the least of their problems. Instead, the attention issues cause the most difficulties for people, especially as they become older and are expected to handle themselves.

One thing that should be evident from the start is that ADHD has nothing to do with intelligence. Some people with ADHD are super smart. Others are above-average, middle-of-the-road, below-average, and slow. Some are university professors, doctors, lawyers, and business titans. There are a lot of regular people. Some people struggle with the basics. You may be anywhere on the IQ scale and still have ADHD. It has nothing to do with intelligence. The other thing to understand is that this is a problem—or a set of problems—with a wide range of characteristics. I would like to describe some of the characteristics of what we call ADHD, give examples, and then talk a bit about what we know and what happens in the brain during ADHD.

One thing to keep in mind is that persons with ADHD frequently complain about having difficulty remaining focused. When they are listening, reading, or working on something, they get a portion of it, but then it drifts off and they are back. Again, they drift off, and they are back. They have a hard time keeping focused. It is comparable to the problem you could experience with a cell phone when in an area with poor reception. You can hear a portion of it, but the message fades in and out.

The other issue is frequent distraction. Like everyone else, they see and hear what is going on around them. They have thoughts running through their minds. Normal people can put that element out of the way and focus on what they need to do, especially if they have something important to complete. People with ADHD find it extremely difficult to do so. They will be sitting in class trying to listen to what is going on, they will be at a meeting or sitting down trying to read or write something; someone drops a pencil, and they will have to check to see where the pencil went. They will then return to their work for a few minutes. They might recall a TV episode they watched the night before, and then they are back at work for a moment. They suddenly remember a conversation they had with someone two hours ago, and they are back on task for a few minutes. Then they are looking out the window, watching a squirrel go up the tree. We all do it, but they do it a little longer than everyone else; they are likely to be checking out the traffic and the cloud formations, the guy mowing the lawn. Then they are back on task for a few minutes, thinking about what they will do after it is finished and how soon this thing will be over.

I have much work to do.

What am I having for dinner tonight?

I am curious, what is on TV tonight?

All of these things come pouring in at once; it is as if you are trying to watch TV and four different stations are streaming at the same time on one channel, making it difficult to distinguish the signal from the noise. However, what is puzzling about this, and what makes it so difficult for others to grasp, is that for people with ADHD, it is happening all the time.

Every person I have ever met with ADHD can do a few things and have no trouble paying attention or focusing. Allow me to give you an example. I noticed a sixteen-year-old boy who was the goaltender for his high school's ice hockey team. Moreover, it just so happened that the day his parents brought him in to see me was the day after his team had just won the state championship in ice hockey, so they were rejoicing about how terrific he was in the tournament the day before. He was a good goaltender. They say he did not miss anything when he was in there playing hockey. Every second of a fast-paced game, he knew where the puck was.

He was completely on top of everything. Every team desires this type of goalie. He was a smart kid and wanted to do well in school. He had hoped to go to medical school. But he was continually getting into mischief with his teachers. They would now and then, "You say things that prove how smart you are. You make very perceptive observations, and it is extremely impressive. But most of the time, you are out to lunch. You are staring out the window right now. You are looking up at the ceiling. You appear to be half-asleep half of the time. You have no idea what page we are on". The question they were asking him over and over was, "If you can pay attention so well, while playing hockey, how come you cannot pay attention in class?"

Here is another case. Parents often bring in their children for observation, and they will say, "You know, the instructor thinks this youngster cannot pay attention for more than five minutes. We all know that is not true. We have seen her play chapter games."

"And she can sit and play chapter games for three hours straight without moving."

"She is easily distracted, according to the teacher."

"That is ridiculous. When she has engaged in those games, She is laser-focused on that television, and the only way to grab her attention is to get in her face or turn off the TV."

Some persons with ADD are very good at most things. They can be into painting, sketching and drawing, and getting really into art. Someone else is used to build engineering wonders using the LEGO bricks they had as a kid. When they are older, they will be tearing automobile engines apart and reassembling them or creating computer networks.

Everyone I have ever encountered with ADHD has a few things they can do where they have no issue paying attention, even if they have a lot of trouble paying attention to practically everything else. And if they ask you about it, you answer:

"What is the deal with this? Why is this so?"

"You can do it there, but not here, here, and here?" Typically, they will say, "It is simple.

"I can pay attention if it is something I am interested in. If not, I will not be able to."

When most individuals hear this, they say, "That is right. Congratulations. That is true for anyone.

"Anyone will pay more attention to something they are interested in than something they are not."

That is correct. But here is the catch.

People who do not have ADHD can typically make themselves pay attention if they have something they must do, and they know they have to do it because it is important, even if very dull. On the other hand, people with ADD have difficulty making themselves pay attention unless the task is highly exciting to them - not because someone told them it should be interesting but because it is interesting to them for whatever reason. Or if they could feel like they have a gun to their head, and something extremely awful is about to happen if they do not take care of the matter right now.

They can concentrate well on some things in certain circumstances. Anything else makes it harder to focus. This is not something that can be controlled voluntarily. It gives the impression of an issue with willpower. "If you can do it here, why not here, here, and here?" But it is not a matter of willpower. It has to do with the way the brain is wired. All of the traits and characteristics of ADHD outlined here are problems that everyone struggles with at times. It is just that folks with ADD have a lot more difficulty with it. In short, ADHD is not an "all-or-nothing situation" like pregnancy, where you either are or are not pregnant. There is not anything in between. It is more like depression, where everyone gets down now and again. But just because someone is miserable for several days does not indicate clinical depression. Only when the depressive symptoms are persistent, causing them trouble, do we say, "That is, indeed, depression. We should do something about it."

As a result, all of the symptoms of ADHD are challenges that everyone encounters from time to time. It is just that people with ADD have a lot more difficulty with it. As stated, the issue is that it is not under voluntary control. It is not something that can be accomplished by the sheer force of will. But let me tell you about some of the other things we notice in ADHD patients. One is that they frequently struggle to get organized to start on projects. For many, arranging their belongings— backpack, desktops, notes, filing system, living space—is more challenging than for most other people (most of the time) unless someone else is assisting them.

Others have no trouble with their belongings but they have difficulty with their time and work. They will tell you, "If I have many things to accomplish at once, it is incredibly difficult to look at it and say, 'OK, that should be first. That should come in second. That should come in third.'" Even when they get their priorities right, which is not always the case, they have trouble getting started.

Another thing you will commonly hear from people with ADHD is that they have difficulty controlling their sleep and alertness. They can't keep up the effort to finish things in a reasonable amount of time. Many people complain about not falling asleep. The3y will tell you, "I frequently stay up much later than I want or should because I have discovered that if I attempt to go to bed until I am fatigued. I just cannot shut my head down. I just keep thinking about things."

"As a result, I stay up late reading, watching TV, surfing the web, or doing anything until I am completely weary. Then I am fine and fall asleep. But the problem is that I sleep like a dead person and have difficulty getting myself up in the morning. And if I do not have someone to assist me to get out of bed in the morning, I am quite likely to be late for whatever I have to do and sleep through it the entire time. So I just keep pushing the snooze button or turning the clock off completely."

During the day, they are usually fine as long as they are moving about or talking. However, if they have to sit still for an extended time to listen, read, or do paperwork, their eyelids become heavy. Another issue that persons with ADHD frequently face is difficulty staying focused on a task. They may begin pretty well, but they struggle to maintain the effort required to complete it. A university track star, a runner came into my office one day and said, "My mind is a wonderful sprinter, but it is a horrible distance runner. If the task I have to accomplish is something I can finish in one quick chunk, I simply go all out for it," he explained. "After that, I am fine. But if it is "something I cannot finish in one swift chunk," it is a longer-term job to chip away at it day after day. And my response has been, "either hurry up and get the thing done or set it aside until becomes an emergency."

Everyone struggles with deadlines from time to time. It is as if people with ADD cannot get started until it becomes an emergency. Another thing that people with ADHD frequently struggle with is writing. Now, I am not talking about penmanship. I am referring to the process of organizing thoughts into sentences and paragraphs. Individuals sometimes say, "I have many ideas for what I should write..." or "For this essay I am expected to write such and such, but it just takes me half an eternity to put the phrases and paragraphs together so they make sense." In short, they have difficulties organizing their thoughts and logically expressing themselves.

Another aspect of ADHD not that part of the official diagnostic criteria is something that many with are concerned about: they frequently struggle with emotion management. But because it is not the same for everyone, I will offer a few examples.

Once a salesman came to me and said, "You know, I was having lunch at the diner yesterday late afternoon. I was in a good mood as I sat there eating my sandwich. The gentleman in the booth behind me finished his lunch. He was munching far too loudly. He was chomping, chomping, chomping." He went on, "There was something about that roar that drove me insane. It was as if a computer virus had infiltrated my mind and devoured all the space, and all I could think about was that noise."

"I was sitting there, hands clenched, genuinely considering going up and punching this guy in the face because he was chewing so obnoxiously loud." But he did not do it as he did not want to go to jail. "But if I had been at home, I would have been yelling at someone or walking out of the room."

"Stuff like that occurs to me a lot," he added. "There will be some minor irritation, the kind of thing that is low on the scale of frustration for most people. It may be a seven, an eight, or a nine for me," he explained. "I sometimes make a big deal out of it. But I am feeling a wave of rage that makes me want to attack someone or damage something. And then it is generally over. It is not always that way," he remarked. "I was in the office the day prior. I was making my way down the hall. My colleague from another department was just around the corner. He was coming toward me, reading papers as he goes. And I had not seen him in quite some time. So, when we approached each other, I came to a halt and said, 'Hey, how are you? 'How are you doing?' I assumed we would come to a halt and talk for a minute, and he looks up, says hello, puts his head down, and continues walking."

"Now, most people would shrug that off in a minute and believe he was in a hurry," he continued. "He might have a meeting or something that he needs to get to. Not for me. It happened during midday. And I was finished for the rest of the day. I spent the entire afternoon questioning myself, did I do something to anger him? Or maybe I did something that irritated someone in his department, and they are all mad at me. Or maybe I am the type of person no one likes, and no one will tell me."

People like this get a notion in their heads about something they want to do or buy and that wish suddenly takes on such great urgency that they feel they have to have it now. It almost does not matter how expensive it is, how inconvenient it will be for them or someone else, or whether they are wasting time and money on something that might be better put off. There is this constant push, and they keep it up until they either get it or hit a brick wall. Even if they obtain it, they are not overjoyed because they are generally off on something else they desire.

One individual mentioned how she was traveling down the interstate, driving in the left lane. She stated, "I was driving in the left lane. The

Jersey barrier was to my left, and an 18-wheeler truck was on my right. We were going around 65 miles per hour when this truck begins to slow down. He did not get into my lane, but it made me think about how enormous this truck was compared to how small my automobile was. And suddenly, I was wondering to myself, what if he did not notice me and pulled over, squishing me into the Jersey barrier? And before I knew it, I was not just thinking about it. I was playing a very vivid movie in my head, imagining exactly what it would look like if that truck came over and smashed into my car, crumpled the car, sharp pieces of metal were sticking into me, I was bleeding to death, the car is being dragged along the Jersey barrier, the truck jackknifes, cars and trucks behind us are hitting us repeatedly, there is this massive traffic jam, it takes a long time to get through I had bled to death by that point. They must notify my family that I have died. And all the while, I was attempting to drive the automobile at 65 mph down the road."

"That sort of thing happens to me all the time. There will be something minor that makes me wonder, what would happen if this happened? Everything is fine and then I am wondering, what would happen if this happened or what would happen if that happened? Before I know it, I am not just thinking about it: it appeals to me."

Not everyone with ADD is obsessive, but they all have that computer virus in the mind thing - that emotion of "I have got to have it now," or "What would happen if?" It comes in and just eats up all the space in their heads, and it is very difficult to put it in perspective, to push it to the back of their minds and get on with what they have to do.

Working memory is very crucial for those with ADHD. "How is your memory?" you may ask someone with ADHD. They will frequently state, "In my family, I have the best memory. I remember things that no one else does." Then they offer an example of a movie they saw ten years ago. They can give you every detail of the whole plot of a movie they saw once and have not seen since.

Or, perhaps, someone will say, "Yeah, I went to the Super Bowl five years ago." Almost every play is still fresh in their mind. Or someone will claim, "I have 450 song" in my head - all the music, lyrics, and verses that were popular in the 1970s." However, even if they are skilled at remembering things from a long time ago, if you ask them about something that happened just a few minutes ago or yesterday, they frequently cannot tell you.

The issue with ADHD is not with long-term storage memory. It has to do with short-term working memory. It is what you rely on when you go into another room to get something, and you are standing there scratching your head, wondering why you came. Or maybe you are working on a project. You go downstairs to grab something for the project, see something interesting or do something else. Soon, you are up to your elbows in project number two, having completely forgotten you were in the middle of project number one upstairs, which was critical to complete.

The teacher will asks the student a question. They will put up their hand and say they have a good answer. Someone else is called on first, however. That student will have to wait while the other kid does their act.

The teacher then says, "What were you going to say?"

It is as though the student is now completely clueless. Not only did I forget what I was going to answer, but what was the question in the first place? Or they will read something and grasp it completely at the time. Then, they read a few more pages, take a breath, and realize their eyes have gone over every word, but they have no idea what they just read. They will study for a test the night before They go over it and if you quiz them, they will know what you are talking about. Then, the next day, they walk into class expecting to obtain a good score, only to discover that a large portion of what they knew the night before has vanished. A few hours or days later, something triggers their recollection, and it all comes flooding back. It is not that they did not have it; it is just that they did not know what to do with it. They could not find it when they needed it.

Perhaps you are getting ready to travel somewhere. You make a list of five items to bring with you. You are walking out the door after half an hour. You have forgotten one of them. You cannot not tell me about the other four. It is a situation in which you must keep one thing in mind while doing another. That is the type of memory impairment that people living with ADHD complain about.

Another aspect of ADHD is active management. It is true that some people, even as adults, are quite restless and anxious. they must always have some part of themselves in motion. Some people, even as adults, are fast to jump into things. And there are undoubtedly many children that suffer from this condition. However, many persons with ADHD struggle with slowing down when they need to slow down and speeding up when it is required. They frequently struggle to keep track of their actions. They will occasionally speak out of turn and fail to consider the consequences. They will do anything without considering, "What would happen if I did this?"

But all of these issues—difficulties with memory, with controlling actions, with regulating emotions, with regulating alertness and sleep, and with being able to focus and shift focus when needed—comprise the range of difficulties that people with ADHD complain about. Keep that in mind that these are all issues that everyone faces from time to time. It is just that folks with ADD struggle with them a lot more. So the question is not whether it occurs at all, but how frequently it occurs.

How much does it interfere with the person's ability to carry out one's daily activities? Why do some people have so much more difficulty than others? Research suggests that it is primarily hereditary. One in every four people diagnosed with ADHD has a parent with it, whether they realize it or not. It was not diagnosed for a long time; even now, it is frequently overlooked. If the afflicted do not have a parent with ADHD, they frequently have a grandmother, an uncle or aunt, a cousin, or a brother or sister.

Some people have it from at a young age. For others, you do not see it much in the early years of schooling, but when they get to middle school and do not have that one teacher who helps them keep things organized, suddenly they must keep track of what is going on in several classes, the homework for different courses and moving from one class to another. They have a lot greater trouble dealing with it on their own.

Some people's parents are so good at building a support system that they do not notice the problem until they get to high school are in their adolescence. But their parents are not aware of what they need to do. Or they move out of the house and go to college or get involved in work where their parents cannot help them. Then you finally realize that you have many problems. But middle school, high school, the first couple of years of college, and then entering the professional world are usually the most difficult times for ADHD people. Those are the periods when they struggle the most. Those are the times when you have the most tasks to complete with the least amount of time.

If you are lucky, as you progress, you will focus more on the things you are strong at and organize the things you are not good at. Some people do fairly well in this manner. However, the same issues can cause significant trouble not only in education but also in how people interact with other family members, manage their social interactions, and handle their careers. We need to figure out how to assist people and work with their abilities while also working around their challenges.

But, to appreciate this, it is necessary to grasp what is going on in the brain. The brain weighs roughly 2.5 pounds: there are 100 billion neurons in there. These are the cells that make up the majority of brain tissue. Most people find it difficult to imagine a number as large as 100 billion, but here is how. Consider pixels on a television screen. Consider a 17-inch TV or monitor screen for your computer. There would be approximately 200,000 pixels on that screen. Imagine if we went to the Freedom Tower in New York after that. It has about 100 floors. Take 17-inch monitor screens and place them side by side, bottom to top, all the way up one side, all the way around, so that this entire building is completely covered with 17-inch TV sets, and turn them all on, adding up all the pixels on all those screens in that entire, massive structure.

If you combined all the pixels, you would have enough to indicate how many neurons one person has in their brain. These neurons, however, are quite small. You must examine them under a microscope. They vary in size and shape, but they all operate on a branch-and-twigs system. And if you isolate any one of them, you will discover that it connects to and interacts with those around it in over 1,000 places. But the most amazing thing is that the entire system operates on low-voltage electrical impulses that are not wired together. That is true for people with ADHD, and it applies to the rest of us as well. They are not linked in any way.

Let me explain how to envision these tiny, microscopic connections that require a microscope to see. It appears to be two mushroom heads butted up against each other. Then there is a space between them that is as thin as a scrap of tissue paper. So everything coming in from the brain, the electrical impulses flowing here, must jump this gap like a spark plug. And there are little receptor buttons on the opposite side with which to communicate. And if it is strong enough...bang. It continues to the next link and then wherever it needs to go. If it does not, it fizzles out. But there are also small bubbles on the side of the container. They are coming from the location where chemicals are created. The brain produces 50 distinct chemicals to aid in the transmission of signals. two of them are in charge of most of the things I have been detailing about ADHD.

So when that electrical impulse occurs, it causes microdots of that chemical to be released. That is what gets over the gap and binds to the receptors. It functions ;like a spark plug. If it reaches the appropriate threshold, it moves on. Then, on this side, some tiny cells act like little vacuum cleaners, sucking back the chemicals and reloading the system. Otherwise, it would be constantly open. We believe that the brains of persons with ADHD produce these chemicals the same way as everyone else. However, they do not efficiently release and reload them.

Another thing we know is that if you give eight out of ten patients with ADHD the proper amount of the right medicine, the system may work better. It makes a tremendous difference for some people. For others, it is significant but not enormous. It helps others a little, but not a lot. Sadly, two out of ten times, it does not work at all.

However, even though this is a chemical issue, ADHD medications cannot fix it completely. It is not like taking a medication when you have a sore throat, and the illness goes away. It is more like my spectacles. My eyes are bothering me. I cannot see very well. When I look at the typewriter-size print, it looks hazy. When I put my glasses on, I can read it just as well as anyone else. If I take them off, I will be right back where

I started. The glasses do not correct my eyes. When I put them on, they help me see better. The same is true with the medications we use to treat ADHD.

It is equally critical to remember that medication is only one necessary treatment for ADHD. There are various ways in which we can assist persons with ADHD in terms of learning skills, using technology, and developing techniques to manage whatever they face in school, on the job, or in their family and social interactions. It is most effective after a very good evaluation in order to understand exactly which problems with ADHD this particular person has. Then the team can start to work. If it is a child, the team consists of the child and the parent, and the doctor. Consultation with educators and teachers working with the child will try to assess their strengths. So this is where we will start.

What are the challenges? What plan can we devise to capitalize on those strengths and assist the child or adult in learning how to handle their obstacles better to thrive and realize their full potential.

Chapter 2:
ADHD Diagnosis

D etermining whether an adult or a child has ADHD is a multi-step process. This chapter will provide an outline of how ADHD is diagnosed. There is no specific test to identify ADHD. For example, many other issues such as sleep disorders, anxiety, depression, and certain forms of learning difficulties also show symptoms similar to ADHD.

If you are concerned that your beloved may have ADHD, the first step is to consult with a healthcare specialist to see if the symptoms match the diagnosis. A mental health expert, such as a psychologist, psychiatrist, or primary care physician, -such as a pediatrician - can make the diagnosis.

AAP (The American Academy of Pediatrics (AAP) suggests that healthcare providers inquire about the child's conduct in various circumstances at home, school, or with peers, parents, teachers, and with other people who care for him or her. The healthcare professional should determine whether the child has another ailment to explain the symptoms or whether they occur concurrently with ADHD.

How is ADHD identified?

To diagnose ADHD, healthcare providers follow the recommendations in the American Psychiatric Association's Diagnostic and Statistical Manual, Fifth Edition (DSM-5)1. This standard diagnostic aids in ensuring that patients with ADHD are properly diagnosed and treated. Using the same criteria across areas also assists in identifying how many children have ADHD and how this disease affects public health.

Here are the criteria in a nutshell. Please bear in mind that they are given for your convenience. ADHD can only be diagnosed and treated by experienced healthcare professionals.

ADHD Criteria in the DSM-5

ADHD individuals have a regular pattern of inattention and/or hyperactivity-impulsivity, which impairs functioning or development including:

Inattention: is diagnosed with 6 (Six) or more symptoms for children under the age of sixteen, or five or more for teenagers and adults aged seventeen and older. The signs of inattention have been present for at least 6 (six) months and are inappropriate for developmental level such as:

- Frequently fails to pay attention to details or makes casual errors in schoolwork, job, or other activities.
- Frequently struggles to focus on chores or play activities.
- When spoken to directly, frequently does not appear to listen.
- Frequently fails to follow directions and fails to complete homework, chores, or workplace duties (e.g., loses focus, sidetracked).
- Frequently struggles with task and activity organization.
- Frequently avoids, hates, or is hesitant to perform things that demand sustained mental effort over a lengthy period (such as schoolwork or homework).
- Frequently misplaces items required for tasks and activities (e.g., school materials, pencils, books, tools, wallets, keys, paperwork, eyeglasses, mobile telephones).
- Is frequently distracted
- Is prone to forgetfulness in regular activities.

Hyperactivity and impulsive behavior: Six or more symptoms of hyperactivity-impulsivity in children under the age of 16, or five or more in teenagers aged 17 and older and adults. Symptoms of hyperactivity-impulsivity have been present for at least 6 (six) months and are disruptive and inappropriate for the person's developmental level:

- Frequently fidgets, taps his or her hands or feet, or squirms in his or her seat.

- Frequently leaves his seat in situations where he is expected to remain seated.
- Frequently runs around or climbs in inappropriate settings (adolescents or adults may be limited to feeling restless).
- Frequently unable to play or participate in leisure activities peacefully.
- Frequently "on the go," operating as though "propelled by a motor."
- He frequently over-communicates.
- Frequently shouts out a response before a question has been fully completed.
- Has a hard time waiting their turn.
- Interrupts or intrudes on others regularly (e.g., butts into conversations or games)

Furthermore, the following conditions must be met:

Before the age of 12 years, several inattentive or hyperactive-impulsive signs have been evident.

- Several symptoms can be found in two or more situations (such as at school, home, or work, with friends or relatives, and in other ventures).
- There is clear evidence that the symptoms interfere with or diminish the quality of social, educational, or occupational functioning.
- Another mental condition does not explain the symptoms (such as a mood disorder, anxiety disorder, dissociative disorder, or personality disorder). In addition, the symptoms do not appear solely throughout a psychotic condition such as schizophrenia.

ADHD can be classified into three sorts (presentations) based on the symptoms:

- Combined Presentation: if both criteria for inattention and hyperactivity-impulsivity were present for at least six months.

- Predominantly Inattentive Presentation: if sufficient symptoms of inattention, but not hyperactivity-impulsivity, have been present for the previous six months.
- Hyperactive-Impulsive personality type: If adequate symptoms of hyperactivity-impulsivity, but not inattention, have been present over the last six months.

Because symptoms might alter over time, the presentation may also shift.

ADHD Diagnosis in Adults

ADHD is a condition that frequently persists into adulthood. To diagnose ADHD in adults and adolescents aged 17 and over, just five symptoms are required, as opposed to the six required in younger children. At older ages, symptoms may appear differently. Adults, for example, may exhibit hyperactivity as excessive restlessness or exhausting others with their energy. Adult ADHD symptoms that commonly cause someone to seek therapy include substantial challenges with job performance, difficulty managing day-to-day obligations such as domestic chores and paying expenses, and stress and worry over an inability to "catch up" to peers.

If you feel that you, your kid, or a loved one has untreated attention deficit hyperactivity disorder (ADHD), getting a diagnosis is a good place to start. While there is no one medical or genetic test for ADHD, a full assessment and physical exam performed by a trained healthcare provider can confirm an ADHD diagnosis.

One of the most frequent neurodevelopmental diseases in children is ADHD. It is frequently detected as a result of classroom disruptions caused by symptoms such as inattention (inability to focus), hyperactivity (moving around excessively or inappropriately for the surroundings), and impulsivity (taking action without thinking through potential consequences). At school, the child appears to be overwhelmed.

According to APA (the American Psychiatric Association), an estimated 5% of children and 2.5 % of adults have ADHD at any given moment.

Many patients with ADHD notice an increase in disturbing symptoms during COVID-19. Although online self-assessment tools can help you determine whether or not you have ADHD-like symptoms, you will need to arrange an in-person session to complete diagnosis and treatment. Meanwhile, read more about what to expect during screening and how to get started if you are diagnosed with ADHD.

Examinations by professionals

During your appointment, a healthcare provider will do the following procedures:

- Inquire about your current symptoms as well as those from your childhood.
- Using diagnostic tools like behavioral rating scales and symptom checklists, he/she will evaluate your symptoms according to DSM-5 criteria. They may request extra interviews with your partner, parent, close friend, or others in some circumstances. They perform a detail physical examination to rule out any other potential causes of symptoms. They also examine for co-occurring or other mental health illnesses such as mood disorder, anxiety disorder, dissociative disorder, or personality disorder.
- Your healthcare professional will inform you whether or not you have ADHD, as well as any other health conditions, at the end of your session. Following that, they will go over treatment options with you and, if necessary, recommend specialists for more screening and care.

An in-depth interview and physical exam by a healthcare specialist can only confirm an ADHD diagnosis. Diagnostic criteria, however, differ slightly depending on whether the patient is an adult or a youngster.

If you are an adult looking for an ADHD evaluation, you must contact a licensed mental health professional such as a clinical psychologist, neurologist, psychiatrist, primary care physician, or social worker.

To determine whether you have ADHD, they will conduct a thorough assessment based on the diagnostic criteria outlined in the American Psychological Association's Diagnostic and Statistical Manual of

Mental Disorders (DSM-5), the national standard for the appropriate diagnosis and treatment of mental health conditions in the United States.

According to DSM-5 and the American Academy of Pediatrics recommendations, healthcare providers such as pediatricians, psychiatrists, and child psychologists can do screening for the diagnose of ADHD in children and adolescents aged 4 to 18. (AAP).

Labs and Examinations

An interview and physical exam are the gold-standard diagnostic procedures for ADHD to uncover ADHD symptoms and any probable mental and physical health issues.

Although you may have heard of many ADHD tests, the illness cannot currently be diagnosed exclusively through brain imaging examinations such as an MRI, PET, or CT scan. However, your doctor may advise for some blood tests, brain imaging examinations, or an electroencephalogram (EEG) to rule out other health issues.

Self-Assessment/At-Home Testing

While many online self-assessments and questionnaires for ADHD symptoms, the majority are not scientifically tested or standardized. As a result, you should not use them to self-diagnose or to diagnose others. Again, to receive a correct diagnosis, you must see a qualified and licensed healthcare provider.

However, if you are unsure whether your symptoms are truly those of ADHD, you can use the World Health Organization's (WHO) Adult Self-Report Scale (ASRS) Screener to identify the signs and symptoms of ADHD in adults.

Children's ADHD Diagnosis

A healthcare provider will conduct the following steps to diagnose a child with ADHD:

- Inquire with the child's parents or guardians, school personnel, and mental health practitioners about any academic or behavioral issues (such as struggles with grades or maintaining friendships)

- To ensure that DSM-5 criteria for an ADHD diagnosis are met, assess the child's symptoms using tools like behavior rating scales or checklists.
- Perform a physical exam and conduct laboratory or other testing to rule out other illnesses that cause similar symptoms, such as seizure disorder, thyroid disorder, sleep disorders, or lead poisoning.
- Additional screening tests for co-occurring or other associated mental health diseases, such as depression, anxiety, learning and language disorders, autistic spectrum disorder, oppositional defiant disorder, conduct disorder, and tic disorders, should be performed.
- Depending on the symptoms, you may require a referral to see a pediatric specialist for additional testing for diseases such as developmental problems or learning difficulties.

While this chapter cannot provide a conclusive diagnosis, it can help you determine whether it is time to seek professional advice for a professional test. According to the Attention Deficit Disorder Association, it should be viewed as a starting point rather than a conclusive diagnostic test (ADDA).

Living with untreated ADHD can be a source of ongoing worry and anxiety for both children and adults. However, while receiving an ADHD diagnosis might be frightening or upsetting, it can also bring new insight into prior challenges, improved self-compassion, and optimism for the future for many people.

Treatment alternatives such as medication, lifestyle adjustments, and coping skills can help you regain control and focus your attention, depending on your specific scenario. It is also crucial to remember that many people with ADHD celebrate the benefits of the illness and that it is possible to live a happy and fulfilling life after being diagnosed with ADHD.

Chapter 3:
Women with ADHD

A ccording to research, ADHD has a higher impact on women than it does on males. Therefore, clinicians need a separate set of tools for identifying and treating the condition in men and women, and women deserve to understand how the disorder impacts them.

According to most mainstream research on attention deficit disorder (ADHD or ADD), there are no significant differences in how the condition manifests in men and women. Data reveals that the sexes have the same type, number, severity of symptoms, the same academic challenges, the same number of comorbid conditions, and the same drug efficacy.

However, the living experiences of real women demonstrate that this is not the entire picture. For example, women with ADHD experience many of the same symptoms as men. Still, they also suffer the additional burdens of rigid gender norms, fluctuating hormones, and a greater predisposition for self-doubt and self-harm. New research shows that while their daily symptoms may be similar, men and women with ADHD have radically different long-term outcomes.

It may be appropriate for the ADHD establishment — and especially women — to accept that gender differences play a much bigger role in ADHD living than previously thought. Here is how we may begin to understand the female ADHD experience.

How Can we Change Our Model to Include More Women?

The earliest definition of ADHD was based on the actions of hyperactive boys. Indeed, until 2013, ADHD was classified as one of the Disruptive Behavior Disorders of Childhood in the Diagnostic and Statistical Manual of Mental Disorders (DSM I-IV). The assumption remains that the ADHD diagnostic criteria apply equally to inattentive women to hyperactive boys. External actions that interfere with other people continue to be the focus of quantitative assessments. However, most women experience an internalized sense of disability, impacting their sense of self and qualitative life management abilities. To account for the most recent data on women's experiences, the conceptual ADHD model must shift from behavior to impairment.

The disparities in presentation and consequences highlight a gap in our increasing understanding of women and ADHD. Women's delicate expressions can be readily misconstrued due to their inattentive symptoms and tend to internalize their feelings. For example, anxiety and/or a mood condition may be used to discount a woman's anguish over unfinished laundry or being late to her child's recital.

The chronic underlying feelings of inadequacy and humiliation, on the other hand, are difficult to accept and describe and even more difficult for clinicians to recognize or quantify. Women trying to hide their differences and are hesitant to ask for help second-guess themselves and retreat when their credibility is called into question.

What Is the Influence of Gender Roles?

Many women believe that complying with gender role standards is the only way to be accepted. The executive functions must be perfectly choreographed to meet societal demands for communication and cooperation. Women with ADHD, on the other hand, are hampered by variable executive functions. Overwhelmed and furious, they realize that they do not have a right to a support system but that they are, in fact, the support system.

Why do Women with ADHD Have a Low Self-Esteem?

Women with ADHD condemn themselves for being distracted and unable to "catch up" with daily duties. They let their lack of drive, disorganization, or tardiness define them, and they expect criticism or rejection as a result. Many people, embarrassed by their emotional reactivity, censor themselves rather than risk incorrect replies. However, when they are less guarded at home, their irritation leads to outbursts directed at partners or children. Such unforeseen consequences leave people disheartened and filled with regret. They attribute these shortcomings to a faulty character in the absence of a neurobiological explanation.

What Role do Hormones Play in ADHD Symptoms?

Monthly hormonal changes begin during puberty, bringing high estrogen and progesterone, increasing neurotransmitters, and improving cognitive ability following menstruation. However, when premenstrual hormone levels fall, women experience an intensification of ADHD symptoms and regular premenstrual changes. Low estrogen causes increased irritation as well as changes in mood, sleep, and attention. Without taking into account underlying ADHD, these apparent symptoms can readily lead to a diagnosis of PMDD.

ADHD symptoms worsen as estrogen levels fall during menopause. Confusion, memory, attention, and sleep become much more affected when combined with age-related cognitive impairments. Given that women now spend around one-third of their lives after menopause, research must investigate the impact of hormone cycles on ADHD symptoms.

Why are Women with ADHD Frequently Perfectionists?

Many women developed self-esteem as a result of early academic accomplishment. As adults, they continue to rely on intellect to compensate, but the difficulty of maintaining focus causes them to doubt their abilities. Success now necessitates massive commitments of time and energy. Despite harsh comparisons to colleagues who appear to achieve effortlessly, they are driven to present a flawless façade, harsh comparisons to colleagues who seem to perform effortlessly. Rigid perfectionism, on the other hand, comes at a heavy cost.

Anxiety fuels a never-ending cycle of self-monitoring. Some ladies spend the majority of the night obsessively preparing for an event. However, when something slips through the cracks, their lofty standards leave them feeling demoralized and unworthy of compassion. Their facade works only if no one suspects the despair that grips them. However, this mask of conformity prevents them from being identified; their difficulties are hidden but no less destructive.

What Role do Comorbid Conditions Play in the Picture?

Most women with ADHD have more than one comorbid condition by maturity, and those symptoms are frequently the most visible. As a result, women are commonly misdiagnosed and treated as having anxiety and mood disorders as primary diagnoses. Their physiological manifestations of anxiety can range from headaches and nausea to nail-biting and cuticle-picking. They are more prone to have dysregulated eating patterns as well as a higher BMI. They are more likely to suffer personality disorders, the most common of which being Borderline Personality Disorder. They may exhibit signs of substance misuse, excessive shopping, or gambling. They may report sensory overload, including hypersensitivity to touch, sound, light, or odors. They are more likely to have been subjected to physical or sexual abuse as children, and they may exhibit PTSD symptoms. Any combination of these comorbid problems creates a complex diagnostic picture.

What are the Possibilities for Undiagnosed Women?

As women's duties grow, so does their psychological pain, yet low self-esteem rarely allows their demands to take precedence. Women with ADHD put off checks and treatments because they are distracted from their self-care, and they function with significant sleep deficits. Inconsistent eating patterns, influenced by inattention and impulsivity, might lead to difficulties. They may rely on prescription medications to manage anxiety, mood disorders, sleep, or pain, or they may self-medicate with alcohol or narcotics if they are chronically stressed.

Women develop and learn to appear less symptomatic, yet their misery remains a closely held secret. They may withdraw from friends and hide their sadness from partners. Because they believe they are unworthy, they may be subjected to mental and physical violence in relationships. When misery is mixed with impulsivity, women commit much more self-harm than males. Even more troubling is their significantly increased risk of suicidal thoughts and attempts. According to recent population research, women with ADHD are more likely to die from accidental causes, particularly accidents.

These dramatically increased risk factors deserve to be addressed as a public health issue. However, these outcomes are avoidable. Healing begins with establishing a secure relationship with one person who serves as a lifeline to acceptance and support.

Messages for Women Suffering from ADHD

Why does ADHD have a considerably higher impact on women. Perhaps a perfect storm of internalized symptoms, hormone cycles, and cultural pressures combine to create an environment of stressors specific to females. Attributing their problems to character flaws promotes the humiliation and demoralization that can damage them. Because women experiencing ADHD are reactive rather than proactive, they gradually lose faith in their own judgment, which repeatedly fails them.

Women with ADHD regard themselves as more disabled than males, and unpleasant situations are more hurtful. They are more prone to blame themselves for their troubles and feel themselves lucky when things go well. They are more likely to experience low self-esteem and feelings of shame. Women with ADHD appear to be more vulnerable than men to their perceived shortcomings in self-regulation. But what if men's experience is not regarded as the gold standard? These differences imply that studies comparing women with ADHD to women without ADHD would provide more detailed information about the impact of ADHD.

We cannot change the wind, but we can adjust the sails. Women with ADHD cannot change their brain wiring, but they can reinterpret their experiences. They can learn to accept their unique skills and abilities, appreciate the creativity of non-linear thinking, set new priorities based on self-acceptance, and thrive in ADHD-friendly surroundings. An ADHD diagnosis, ideally, is the first step in changing a harmful belief system: it provides a biological explanation for why things are so difficult and affirmation that helps them own their triumphs.

Chapter 4:
Co-occurring conditions with ADHD

M illions of adults suffer with attention deficit hyperactivity disorder (ADHD). ADHD can result in persistent exhaustion, worry, disorganization, and problems at work and home in the absence of education and therapy. Hyperactivity disorder is a condition in which an individual may have many attention symptoms such as difficulties focusing or hyperactive and impulsive. Because it is a developmental condition, some symptoms must appear throughout childhood. Although, for many people, they can cope until they become older, and the task demands of daily life get larger.

What makes this different from ADD? ADD was an older term used in early versions of the DSM. ADD did not have the hyperactive-impulsive news traits, but they discovered that they were associated after much research. So, it is essentially a subset of the same illness, albeit some people have ADHD but are inattentive, meaning they do not exhibit hyperactivity or impulsive behavior. Then some are hyperactive-impulsive rather than inattentive.

While fewer people are like that, a good number have the combined symptoms of inattention, impulsivity, and hyperactivity. What are some prevalent misconceptions among adults who feel they have ADHD or have been diagnosed with it? I believe that everyone believes they have ADHD and have been on the spectrum at some point in their lives. However, if you only have inattentiveness on occasion but it does not affect your functioning and are not overly concerned about it, you will not be eligible for the ADHD diagnosis. Adult ADHD has a prevalence incidence that is half that of childhood ADHD. So, according to national surveys, ADHD affects around 5% of the population in childhood and 2.5% of the population in adults. As a result, around half of persons recover from ADHD by 18, while the other half continue to endure symptoms throughout]adulthood. I believe a major myth is that it looks the same in maturity because it does not. ADHD's hyperactive and impulsive qualities look completely different in a child.

A child is running around the classroom, getting out of his seat, which attracts negative attention. It is normal that the teacher will fight them and talk to the parents about "restlessness". As adults, we are a little more controlled in terms of our behavior, so we are not going to be running around when we know we are not supposed to, but you might feel fidgety. We see people tapping very nervously on a desk or table; that could be a manifestation of an adulthood form of combined ADHD.

Now we will go into the diagnostic procedure and the DSM criteria for ADHD, but as mentioned earlier, many individuals believe they have ADHD because they cannot sit down and read a book for more than an hour or cannot focus on having a discussion. When is it ADHD and when is it simply a lack of interest in whatever is going on? I believe this is even more perplexing because our culture currently promotes a lot of inattentiveness. Several things are demanding our attention in these days of multi-tasking; many studies suggest that the more frequently you are on social media, the more you start to exhibit signs. This does not imply that social media causes ADHD, but it does mean that you will become more inattentive.

I was watching news the other day when I realized that not only are the newscasters talking, but there is a little ticker on the bottom rolling with more statistics. There are pop-ups in the corner, and two of the folks I was watching the news with were also looking at the CNN app at the same time. A lot of things are competing for our attention. So, everyone has ADHD from time to time, but when you have the clinical symptoms, it is different; in an adult, there is a lot of emotional dysregulation going on, making it more difficult to tolerate irritation. They might be a lot less patient. It may be much more difficult to prepare ahead and organize themselves. As a result, they are always chaotic and muddled in their heads. Once again, this is not something that happens once in a while when you have a busy day or a week; it is something that happens regularly that reduces your quality of life and may even impair relationships. In fact, one of the most common complaints of adulthood ADHD is difficulty in relationships, whether with friends or romantic partners. Because, as you can expect, if you are not paying attention to your spouse, you are constantly asking for repetition, and your partner becomes very irritated with you, saying, "You never listen to me, you are always focusing on yourself." This can cause many problems in their relationships.

What are some of the most prevalent co-occurring conditions with ADHD?

Depression is the most prevalent co-occurring disorder with ADHD. It has been well-established and documented in the literature for persons with both childhood and adult ADHD. As a result of underperforming in school due to being diagnosed with ADHD, people begin to acquire anxiety, another typical co-occurring disorder. Anxiety is nearly always secondary to ADHD because ADHD makes them feel inept, such that they develop performance anxiety and feelings of inadequacy, which then contribute to the anxiety symptoms that eventually become clinical.

There is also a subset of ADHD children and adults with substance disorders; therefore, people who have ADHD are more prone to experiment with drugs or alcohol later in life. In addition, they are more likely to experiment with substances than their classmates, and as adults, they are more prone to have a problem with substance abuse.

Another major correlated aspect, in my opinion, is that adults with ADHD have a higher risk of suicide ideation than the general population. As a result, they are predisposed to a variety of psychological illnesses, and they are frequently comorbid with other types of learning disabilities. Again, it can be difficult to determine whether the learning handicap is a separate condition or if ADHD causes learning difficulties. It stems from their inability to pay attention, resulting from which they have not absorbed the information they should have by a given age or grade.

Suppose I am an adult and have been diagnosed with both depression and ADHD. Should I treat one first or both simultaneously? I believe it is usually beneficial to address both at the same time. Because by that point, I believe adults have seen the interaction between those two variables. They reinforce each other. ADHD causes additional emotional dysregulation, which may include mood dysregulation, and mood dysregulation exacerbates ADHD. One of the symptoms of depression, which not everyone has - but some do - is difficulty making decisions and concentrating. So, if someone additionally has ADHD, it would be interesting to determine from where that attention problem stems. Is it related to sadness or ADHD? Perhaps it is not all that important. It is just that they are related and treating both simultaneously is the best path ahead. When adults present with ADHD, they have untreated ADHD. As a result, untreated ADHD in adults can wreak havoc on their lives.

It is tough for them to stay determined to improve, avoid problems at work, and keep their jobs. In reality, I have discovered that many adults with ADHD have organized their work-life so that ADHD is less noticeable. Many adults with ADHD become their own bosses because no one is disciplining them; they must, however, discipline themselves. It may impede their level of performance, but if they operate their own business or are entrepreneurs running their own firm, I occasionally find folks with ADHD fielding out duties they are not particularly good at. Because of their ADHD symptoms, others can work on it for them, and now they can then focus on the types of jobs they truly want to perform themselves. The catch, of course, is that people with adult ADHD do not like schedules, so they tend to work in more entrepreneurial types of jobs, where they can wake up and start working when they want to, and maybe they will work at night too; but it is all on their own time.

However, it can occasionally aggravate ADHD because people with ADHD require structure and may be attempting to design their lives around their illness. Sometimes they make those symptoms a little more difficult to control because they are not sleeping at the proper time an d they are up at all hours; this interferes with their next day and the productivity and attention they require. So, sleep disorder is another issue. ADHD may co-occur with one or more other conditions.

The oppositional-defiant disorder affects around 40% of people with ADHD (ODD). A habit of fighting characterizes ODD, losing one's temper, refusing to follow the rules, blaming others, purposefully irritating others, and being angry, resentful, spiteful, and vindictive.

Conduct disorder (CD) is common in people with ADHD, affecting 27 percent of children, 45–50 percent of adolescents, and 20–25 percent of adults. Children with conduct disorder may be hostile toward people or animals, destroy property, lie or steal from others, run away, miss school, or violating curfews. In addition, adults with CD frequently engage in acts that land them in hot water with the authorities.

In adults, roughly 38% of ADHD patients also have a mood condition. Significant mood swings distinguish mood disorders. Children with mood problems may appear to be in a terrible mood all of the time. For example, they may cry every day or be irritated with others for no apparent cause. Mania, Depression, and bipolar disorder are examples of mood disorders.

Approximately 14% of children with ADHD are also depressed, whereas just 1% of children without ADHD are depressed. Roughly 47 percent of persons with ADHD also have depression. ADHD is usually the first symptom, followed by depression. Environmental and genetic factors both play a role.

Up to 20% of people with ADHD may exhibit symptoms of bipolar disorder, a severe condition characterized by moments of mania, unusually heightened mood and activity, followed by episodes of clinical despair. Bipolar disorder, if left untreated, can harm relationships and lead to job loss, educational issues, and even suicide.

Anxiety disorders can affect up to 30% of children and up to 53% of adults with ADHD. Patients with anxiety disorders frequently worry excessively about various things (school, work, etc.) and may feel tense, edgy, stressed out, tired, anxious, and have difficulty sleeping.

Tics or Tourette Syndrome affect less than 10% of persons with ADHD, but Tourette Syndrome affects 60 to 80% of those with ADHD. Tics are characterized by sudden, fast, recurring, involuntary movements or vocalizations. Tourette Syndrome is a considerably rarer but more severe tic disorder. People make noises, such as yelling a phrase or sound, and movements, such as repetitive flinching or eye blinking, almost every day for years.

Up to 50% of children with ADHD also have a learning disorder, whereas only 5% of children without ADHD have learning disorders. Learning impairments can interfere with how people absorb and apply new information, such as reading or calculating. Dyslexia and dyscalculia are the most frequent learning disabilities. Furthermore, 12 percent of children with ADHD have speech impairments, compared to 3 percent of children without ADHD.

Chapter 5:
Adult ADHD & Relationships

I am aware that all these facts about ADHDA are gloomy. But, you know, sometimes you must tackle an issue head-on to become a champion, win, and make the best of a bad circumstance. If you deny it or put a sugar coating on it, you will not be remarkably successful in dealing with actual ADHD difficulties. And I believe in tackling things head-on.

What about everyone else: the folks who do not have access to all these resources and are not as well educated? This implies that there is not much ADHD awareness out there because it can be difficult to penetrate mainstream media at times. Unfortunately, people do not take it seriously. Many have responded, "Oh yeah, we know about ADHD– it is a gift..." and all you have to do is find the proper spouse to enjoy life with them, as well as the right work to be grateful for. But I said to myself, "Well, it is not quite that straightforward."

So let us talk about it to discover if ADHD is the elephant in your relationship's room.

ADHD is the elephant in the room of society, therapists, job offices, but especially the elephant in the space of relationships. If you go to a couples' therapist, they will often focus on communication and all the usual things that couples therapists do. However, if they overlook ADHD, you are losing a vital aspect. That is why it is not about one spouse being the one to blame; it is about the idea that we are missing a third entity, which is significant in the relationship, and that is ADHD.

Many couples are locked in an unpleasant parent-child relationship, with the non-ADHD partner playing the parent and the ADHD partner playing the child. It frequently begins when the partner with ADHD fails to complete chores, such as failing to pay the cable bill, leaving clean laundry on the bed, or leaving the kids stranded after offering to pick them up. Then, the non-ADHD partner gradually accepts more and more home tasks.

They become more bitter as the partnership becomes more unbalanced. It becomes more difficult to recognize and appreciate the ADHD spouse's positive features and contributions. Of course, the ADHD partner is aware of this. Instead of putting in any effort, they view their non-ADHD partner as a burden difficult to please.

You may feel ignored and lonely if your companion has ADD. Your partner can concentrate on topics that are of interest to them but not to you. They never seem to follow through on their promises. They may appear to act more like a child than an adult. You irritate them, and you've grown to despise the person you've become. You're simply going to fight, or you're going to stay quiet. Worse, you're worried about being saddled with domestic obligations while your partner has all the fun.

If you have ADHD, you might think your partner has turned into a nagging monster. The person you cared about has turned into a control freak, attempting to regulate and control every minute of your life. You can't meet your partner's expectations no matter how hard you try. The simplest approach to cope with them is to ignore them.

Either of these events can lead to the end of a relationship. If any of the above characteristics sound familiar, your relationship may be suffering from what I refer to as the ADHD impact. ADHD symptoms, as well as your reactions to them, have harmed your relationship. The good news is that knowing the effects of ADHD in your relationship can help you turn it around. You can reconstruct your life if you learn to recognize the obstacles ADHD brings to relationships and the steps you may take to address them.

ADHD symptoms that might lead to relationship issues:

Having difficulty paying attention

If you have ADHD, you may find yourself zoning out during talks, making your spouse feel ignored and undervalued. You may also overlook critical information or agree to something you later regret, which can aggravate your loved one.

Forgetfulness

Even though a person with ADHD is paying attention, they may forget what was promised or discussed later. So when it comes to your spouse's birthday or the formula you planned to pick up, your partner may start to suspect that you are untrustworthy or don't care.

Organizational abilities are lacking

This can result in difficulties completing duties as well as general household turmoil. It's not uncommon for a partner to feel like they're constantly cleaning up after the person with ADHD, and that they're shouldering excessive family duties.

Impulsivity

When you have ADHD, you may say things without thinking, which can lead to wounded emotions. Unfortunately, this impulsivity can also lead to irresponsible and even reckless behavior (for example, buying a large purchase not in the budget, resulting in financial arguments).

Excessive emotional outbursts

Many persons with ADHD have difficulty controlling their emotions. You may be easily irritated and have a problem discussing matters calmly. Your partner may feel as if they must walk on eggshells to avoid a meltdown.

Understanding the role of ADHD in your relationship is the first step toward transforming it. Once you've identified how ADHD symptoms influence your relationships as a pair, you'll be able to discover better methods to respond. For the ADHD partner, this requires learning how to manage their symptoms. This includes knowing how to react to frustrations in ways that inspire and motivate the non-ADHD partner.

It's simple to see how feelings on both sides of the relationship might contribute to a harmful cycle. The non-ADHD partner criticizes, nags, and grows progressively resentful, while the ADHD partner feels defensive and withdraws, feeling judged and misunderstood. Of course, nobody is happy in the end. But this does not have to be the case. Learn about the role ADHD plays in your relationship and how both of you may choose more positive, better, and productive ways to respond to obstacles and communicate with each other to create a healthier, happier relationship. With these tactics, you may improve your relationship and bring you both closer together.

Chapter 6:
The Effect on the Partners of Adults with ADHD

A lthough it is not a scientific concept, I want to discuss something: you will not find it in any DSM; *it is ADHD's double-triple-whammy.* It all starts with a late-diagnosed adult with ADHD. So, by late-to-diagnosis, I mean an adult who does not realize he or she has ADHD until their 30s – maybe their 20s, 30s, 40s. I have known people in their 80s who have had their initial diagnosis.

What do they all have in common? It is a three-layer effect, their triple whammy.

It Starts with **ADHD neurobiology,** *then adds* **undiagnosed ADHD symptoms,** *which are often misread and generate* **negative feedback** *from childhood. So, you get a lot of bad comments, and* **negative thought patterns will develop.** *You will develop bad attitudes toward yourself and, more often, against other people because people can be incredibly unfair. Negative thoughts result in* **poor coping mechanisms.**

So what are some of these neurological characteristics?

So If we took the symptoms from the DSM, or the diagnostic criteria, and rate them in terms of how common they are in ADHD relationships, at the top, we will find: easily get distracted, has difficulty organizing tasks and activities, has difficulty sustaining tasks or attention and tasks, is forgetful in everyday obligations, and loses things needed for tasks and activities. But if we look at the bottom, we see: he feels on the move or driven by the motor, he talks excessively, leaves his seat in situations, and recedes as expected. So, these hyperactive symptoms are not as common, but they are the symptoms that many people associate with ADD.

We can say grownups cannot have it because for us, ADHD is that little child across the street who could not keep his mouth shut and was always running around and sometimes running out in the street, worrying his mother to death. But all I knew was that I did not know much about it. I believe that is true for many of us. We do not grasp the main idea of ADHD in adults.

Bad comments

There are always misinterpretations and people with ADHD get bad responses. For example, people with ADHD are scattered or absent-minded, have immaturity, dysfunctional family background, selfishness, passiveness, laziness, or introversion. This is a major one: passive aggressive.

Another most important aspect is organization, which means organizing yourself around the house, whether you are a lady or a male with ADHD. How organized is your home? How well-organized are you when it comes to getting ready for work in the morning? How well do you organize yourself at work? How well-organized are you in terms of achieving your objectives over time?

Are you taking each step, or are you just reacting to whatever stimuli come your way? If we talk about starting and finishing tasks, some men with ADD appear to like home improvement projects. But is it always completed? Not always, to be sure.

The afflicted is not a good listener. Listening skills require focusing on what someone is saying when they say it rather than listening to all of the other channels running in your thoughts.

Mood and temper is another one that most people do not understand. I believe that is why many people get misdiagnosed as bipolar because of irritability and rage issues.

Sleep can be quite difficult for those with ADD. Going to sleep is perhaps the dullest and tedious thing you can do. You go into bed and lie there, waiting for nothing to happen. That does not jive well with ADHD wiring.

Cooperating, being relax and sit quietly is at the bottom of the list.

So, what are some examples of bad mindsets/negative thoughts?

"When I am successful, it is because of chance!"

It is as if it simply occurred since they do not always recall the steps they took to get to that point of advancement, and they do not believe they can do it again. So, people with ADHD think they just got lucky.

Adults with ADHD experience a lot of imposter syndrome.

"I am less worthy than others, and I always make mistakes" – ADHD has an "always-never" mentality.

Dr. Barkley describes it as a dysregulation condition, which means that there is often underdoing and overdoing, and there is not a lot of gray areas, so it is like, "I always make mistakes."

Or there is the ADD person in complete denial who says, "I never make mistakes; it is everyone else who has a problem!"

"I have no control over my life; the world is unjust to me." When they think about it, especially if they have undiagnosed ADD, the world appears to be unfair.

"Everyone is usually furious with me," and "I am doubtful that things will ever change..."

What are your coping tactics going to be if you have those kinds of mindsets?

Frankly, if you have these mindsets, you must give credit to anyone who can get out of bed every day and fight the good fight because a lot of us would simply collapse and say, never mind.

So, here are some examples of inadequate coping strategies:

First is denying and downplaying: "Oh, the scratch in the car is not all that awful" or "I did not go bankrupt that much!"

There are so many different methods to deny and minimize. Take the concept of having the discussion later

That is the same thing. "We will talk about that later, honey," he says. That also means never. When you think about it, these coping tactics appear quite rational because the person with ADD knows that if they try to have a conversation, it will not go well. Maybe they will not focus on understanding what their spouse wants or doing things better the next time. So, what was the point of going there in the first place? It simply does not make sense.

The third one is quitting: some persons with ADD will simply walk away from a relationship. They will not even understand why they are leaving. They only know something is wrong, and they do not know why, so they will leave. The same goes for rationalizing and blaming, as well as quitting a job. It is like saying, "I have had it! I am done."

The fourth one is controlling: individuals who are experiencing a lot of turmoil may react by exercising control. But, again, having a rigidly scheduled calendar or routine is a smart strategy if you tend to go into chaos or disorganization. Still, the problem comes when something upsets the routine and you cannot cope; you cannot adapt or be flexible, so it might work when you are single, but then you get married, have a child, get promoted at work, or something else happens.

The fifth is aggressive: when you lack the internal motivation initiation, you may subconsciously come up with all kinds of ways to get yourself inspired and being hostile is something that summons energy. Rushing through jobs and activities can be fun to hurry through them, even if you make mistakes along the way.

For adults with ADHD, this is a triple whammy. At the same time, their partners are riding the roller coaster and experiencing these ups and downs. When you find your partner has some peculiarities, the first dip on the roller coaster occurs. Maybe you did not see it at first because the dopamine was flowing with all those feel-good hormones and that new love and the novelty and excitement of the pursuit and everything else. But then it settles down into a rhythm, and things begin to happen. You realize you had a conversation, but your ADHD partner does not seem to remember it or does not remember it in the same way you do. Perhaps you state, "Okay, we are not going to get that massive flat-screen television." What my spouse may have overheard was, "Go ahead and purchase that flat-screen TV. Because of his "wiring," he could hear whatever he chose to listen to. It was incredible. And I had faith that he would listen to it.

Brain signals, like words, begin as sound signals and go to our ears, where they are transformed into electrical, chemical messages based on dopamine and norepinephrine. Then they go through all of the brain's circuits to the auditory cortex, where they are processed. This is where we interpret what we hear. So, if we cannot understand the words "No, we cannot afford that widescreen TV," the cortex will not listen to it. So, in the next stage...you could say, "So, I will attempt to control the unmanageable here. I am an organized person. I keep track of everything." So, what if my partner is unable to process the mail or forgets to pay the bills? I can do it, and that is fine. But the truth is each partner brings something unique to the relationship. It is not a one-sided path.

However, as time passes, it might become increasingly difficult to handle some of the commotions. It can become difficult to foresee, and then it can be broken down into a stress-related illness like anxiousness. Depression, fibromyalgia, and hypertension are all common conditions, especially in females. Many males who are married to ADHD women suffer from depression and insomnia.

And what happens when the first, second, or third baby arrives, especially if that baby has ADHD too and your partner's bad coping strategies are still there. Again, denying and minimizing are very common all over the place. You have no idea what is going on, and you keep attempting to fit it into your previous paradigms of what it could be.

"Oh, she is working too hard."

"Oh, he has not gotten used to having a new baby."

"Oh, he did not learn all of these things as a child."

As one of my clients said, "I used to believe, my husband did not learn these things because he was an only kid, and maybe being an only child means you do not have to perform as many duties. As a result, I attempted to mimic some of these habits in housework. I expected him to "pick up"!

However, persons with ADHD can watch it but do not catch onto the behaviors and learn from them. As a result, you begin to tolerate dysfunctional behaviors—anything to keep things running smoothly. You get to the point where it is easier for you to take out the garbage instead of arguing with your partner about it one more time. If your companion has ADHD and is irritable, you start walking on eggshells. To avert a crisis, you may become overly attentive and controlling.

But you already know that crises are much better handled if they can be avoided rather than dealt with after the fact. So, you are just waiting to see what your spouse will do; you are attempting to prevent it from happening. Then you can begin to blame your ADHD partner: "You are self-centered. You are irresponsible. You are solely concerned about yourself." Alternatively, you may blame yourself for not noticing these things sooner. It is easy to get twisted up when you are furious all the time. Some persons with ADHD are skilled at provoking, which is a subconscious way of getting the adrenaline pumping and self-medicate. As a result, their partners may get provoked. I have seen typically calm folks who had never been upset until this point in their lives become angry—yelling and occasionally violently tossing objects.

"I threw a coffee table!" exclaimed one lady, hesitantly. You had the impression that she would never have thought that before in her life, but she would become so worried and irritated.

However, if you have ADHD, all you know is that your partner is constantly going crazy and off: you believe your partner is the source of the problem. But you are both struggling with ADHD and are not even aware of it. So, the relationship suffers a triple whammy: undiagnosed symptoms combined with poor coping skills on both sides means negative feedback for both partners: "You are selfish!" or "Well, you are a shrieking banshee!" You may switch back and forth. As a result, couples form negative perceptions of their relationship and themselves.

Finally, pessimistic thinking results in even worse coping mechanisms.

Conflict is something we hear a lot about. There is much arguing going on. Some people with ADHD will be quite defensive in the face of criticism. In addition, they have the impression that they are parenting a second child.

One of my favorite books is by Dr. Margaret Weiss, her mother, Dr. Gabriel Weiss, and Dr. Hecht man. "ADHD in Adulthood: A Guide to Current Theory, Diagnosis, and Treatment." is a fantastic book. Here is what they state about denial: "Individuals with ADHD are ignorant of the activities that cause others to respond negatively. They are aware, though, that others are nagging them. Yet, the link between their actions and this nagging response remains a mystery. While the patients tune out, the white noise of nagging becomes a more distant hum."

Meanwhile, their families ratchet up the heat, becoming even more irritable and domineering; this is a rather typical occurrence. If you go to couples therapy with that pattern, they will miss the ADHD and see the angry and controlling partner. They will say, "If you simply stop controlling, your partner will step up to the plate." But you did not always become domineering because you wanted to. While I am sure it happens, many people are compelled to play that role.

What about co-parenting with an ADHD adult? Kids, of course, adore their parents. However, according to the ADHD Partner Survey respondents, it can be tough because the ADHD spouses are loving, sensitive parents. However, there are issues because the partner with ADHD frequently likes to have fun and lacks discipline. This creates a difficulty since the partner who does not have ADHD is perceived as the heavy, or the enforcer.

What occurs is that some individuals with ADHD discover they are not very good at enforcing discipline. They will be either too soft or too firm. They will both overdo and underdo it. Again, it is because of the regulation; therefore, they have learned to avoid it. It is a little simpler to have fun, but it causes difficulty in the relationship. The partner with

ADHD may also lose his or her anger with the child, resulting in slaps, hits, or verbal abuse.

It is not uncommon to learn that it is the same thing that people with ADHD received as children. Instead of understanding their ADHD child, they will repeat what was stated to them. You are self-centered. You are lazy. You only do what you desire. You do things because YOU WANT TO. Because they think it is beneficial, even though it has not helped them, they do not know what else to do as we do not, they do not know ADHD.

Chapter 7:
How the Non-ADHD Partner Can Better Handle the Relationship

I t is not just about challenges at school or work. It really encompasses the entire life of someone with ADHD. We really need to recognize all those other areas and look at how we can use the same skills. An intimate relationship is much more complex say than managing a school project. There are a lot more pieces to it, which is why we are talking about it.

The need to talk about it is not always acknowledged. Sadly, that is still the case today; not a lot of people out there can speak specifically to a partner who does not have ADHD in the relationship. And many of us are very surprised about the impact of ADHD on the relationship and the partner who has been living with it.

But still, books and information about ADHD are lacking. Nothing really the impact on the relationship. It is not just school or work or social interactions. Relationships are a huge part of life. A couple definitely is a different dynamic with different expectations. You might know someone who works in the same space or is a social friend. Obviously, ADHD does not have the same impact on all relationships whether these individuals are just dating or about to be married. It rears its ugly head later on when you get past the fun stuff and into the day-to-day living, where it shows up more and surprises the both of you.

I can acknowledge you as the non-ADHD partner, but not really look at you as a separate person in need of support. It is about how you support your partner. there are things we can do to help them manage their ADHD. But in the end, you are a half of a relationship that deserves to have your support. Remember that these challenges are unique to your situation. Some books and therapists acknowledge the varied aspects of ADHD. But they tend to focus more on the relationship as a couple, characteristic of couples therapy. It does bring awareness of how ADHD shows up but does not serve to treat the afflicted partner.

This leads to the question, what if your partner is not ready to go there yet?

By acknowledging the impact of ADHD, accepting them as the part of you that needs to be actively managed, some people are in a better space than others. Some are on a journey to discover themselves when they may not be ready to deal with the condition. It is one of those interesting dynamics that add complexity to the relationship. Relationships, in general, are already complex because they are meshing people's challenges and strengths together. Then we add in this third element, called ADHD, which throws everything into a whole different space. And if your partner is not ready to acknowledge it and actively do anything about it, where does that leave you, as the non-ADHD partner?

Often, it feels like you are just kind of hanging, right? You have no control and are dependent on them to be ready to take those next steps. Maybe "tomorrow" will be years from now, who knows? So, in the meantime, what if we took control of what we can control. You say to yourself, awhile my focus is on looking at the choices we have in a relationship, we have chosen to be in this one. We are staying because there are obviously several reasons to stay. But we do have a choice. So, ADHD partners should be looking at what they can choose and what changes they can make.

If you were in a relationship where you can control your partner, chances are you would not want to be in that relationship. We want an equal partnership. We do not want to pretend that we have no control over our lives. ADHD partners are unique in that they are focused on the other individual as part of the relationship and what steps can actively be taken to improv life, reduce stress, acknowledge the impact, and get the support needed.

The National Institute of Health lists the functions relevant to marital harmony. A partner can be more challenging to get along with as well as less dependable and more likely to act on impulse. Every individual has strengths and challenges, but not everybody has marital function issues or ADHD. They do not apply to everyone so society is confused. However, it does not come as a surprise that struggles exist in most relationships, whatever the cause. Pretty much anyone with ADHD is going to have marital function (part of executive functions) challenges but it is not vice versa. But they can still cause several issues.

Common challenges show up when somebody has ADHD at levels of deficit. It can pertain to any or all of the following: organizing and prioritization, getting started on something, focusing and sustaining attention on tasks, regulating alertness, staying focused, processing, speed of action, managing frustrations, utilizing working memory, and accessing recall. Think about your day-to-day tasks and living with these challenges. What would it mean to your relationship? What do those common expectation we have of a relationship look like?

The challenges are many: if you are put them in the context of relationship, it spells trouble. Issues emerge if we do not have an understanding of the partner with ADHD. They may have the perception that they are being ignored and your commitment does not really mean that much to you. So there is a general lack or mutual support. If you add in the perspective of out of sight out of mind, the emotions shift. One of the partners may no longer care about the relationship or are waiting for improvements.

When talking about emotions, they may be positive or negative. Your partner becomes really excited about things they had not looked at before, which is exciting and makes you see things through different eyes; but they can also get emotional and to a higher level than you. When they are frustrated and upset, and things do not go their way, quick, strong emotions emerge. This may or may not dissipate. They can just walk away from or the emotions will linger as the rumination starts.

So often, you are the non-ADHD partner, looking to support your partner and help them manage their emotions to make them feel better. It can lead to suppressing harmful emotions. You meet them at their level which is likely higher than yours. You help your partner through the stress and distress so the relationship can become healthy again. It can be a pattern that needs to be addressed continually.

Another problem is the lack of future awareness. If your partner does not have foresight, they are not thinking about the future. It is considered outside what they are living in the moment. It could pertain to the household budget, saving for retirement, meeting bill payments on time, etc. account. Obviously, something is going to cause conflict in the relationship, leading to not really fully trusting them, feeling like you need to question their decisions. It could be about missing money or overspending impulsively.

Not taking ownership of one's mistakes is common, especially if you think of ADHD as a negative. Are you then to blame. But you have been told all your life that you are not tried hard enough and you are not doing it right. Your self-esteem takes a hit, while will impact how you react in critical times. It is common to deflect ownership of mistakes and put them on someone else to protect yourself.

So it is hard for the non-ADHD partner, especially when communication fails. You may not understand where the emotion is coming from when it is an issue of not taking ownership. You want the relationship to work and you enjoy your partner. You want to make things right in the face of the challenges of ADHD. It takes two to work on the relationship. But taking ownership is an essential step. We cannot control our partners but appreciate when they accept responsibility. Now the couple can go to a better place and higher level of quality of life.

The challenge is to focus on what we can control. So, take a deep breath and think about a situation that has happened in your relationship, maybe a common irritant that occurs quite frequently. Maybe there is more than ADHD involved in there.

The example can be something somewhat small, but is a common frustration and conflict in the relationship. I want you to go 500 feet up and take a bird's eye view. You have removed yourself but are still viewing the situation. You are no longer as invested in the emotions and the dynamics because you are looking at it from a broader perspective. It should alter your perspective of what is going on. The way you approach the situation and what you can you control might be different now that you are above the surface.

Even if the partner is truly living in the moment, and it is a matter of out of sight out of mind, they likely do not have full awareness. They might not even know why you are upset. They do not remember that they promised to pick up the milk, so they have no idea why you are not happy.

How might that change? How would you approach it? What can you control about this particular situation that would move it towards the kind of relationship that you want?

Go ahead and write down a few of thoughts. This is the beginning of the process. We are starting to peel back those layers of awareness and understanding. Once you start planting those seeds, they will naturally start opening up and shifting a little bit the next time that same situation comes around. Play with different reactions or things you can control that came to mind during that exercise. try them on and see what happens. See what reaction you get from your partner. If it is different and positive, it will lead to a better dialogue and less stressful dynamic at that moment.

Remember, there is no simple formula to a successful marriage. Whether you are married to someone with or without ADHD, there is no one method; but there certainly are some things you can do to help improve the quality of the marriage.

Here are ten helpful hints for keeping the romance alive and balancing each other out. A happy marriage requires effort. Unfortunately, a good marriage with an ADHD partner needs more effort.

1. Research ADHD. There are numerous outstanding books on the subject. The more you learn about ADHD, the more you will understand your partner. Obviously, no two people with ADHD are alike, but there are some similarities to be aware of.

2. Do not make a "moral diagnosis", attributing ADHD-related bad behaviors to a lack of motivation or effort. For example, if your spouse says he will take out the garbage and then goes right past it, do not believe he did it on purpose, was disrespectful or passively hostile. When he skips specifics or forgets essential duties, do not believe he is

selfish or does not care about you. All of this is part of the ADHD bundle. A moral diagnosis aggravates the situation.

3. Do not treat your spouse like a child if they have ADHD. This is unromantic and exacerbates both parties' problems and resentments.

4. Make regular time for talk at least a half-hour every week at the same time and in the same place. Choose a time when you know you will be able to sit down and make plans, establish rules and habits, and work through obstacles. It is critical to communicate clearly. Many couples only "communicate" when they are bickering or fighting. Understanding comes from constant communication, which inevitably leads to empathy and closeness.

5. When it comes to intimacy, do not forget to make love. People are so busy these days, whether they have ADHD or not, that sex typically falls to the bottom of their priority list. Yet, lovemaking is one of the few human acts that is both enjoyable and beneficial. So do it as often as possible. Set up dates for coupling. Anticipation is a type of foreplay.

6. Establish a division of work in which each partner performs what he or she excels at. For example, you are terrible at accounting and despise dealing with money and someone has to pay the bills. On the other hand, your husband enjoys managing money and is adept at keeping track of it, so leave everything to him.

7. This brings us to another crucial point. If you are the one with ADHD, be grateful for your spouse's coaching and "honey-do" lists. Consider the lists as helpful reminders rather than irritating reminders. To keep their lives on track, people with ADHD require reminders, structure, routines, and timetables.

8. Ensure that your partner understands your situation. The ADHD spouse is sometimes unaware of the influence his activities have on his partner. His intentions are good, but the consequences of his acts are frequently negative. Explain this to him during one of your regular communication sessions, and not during a fight.

9. Have fun together by doing the things you both enjoy. Having happy times makes it much simpler to get through the bad times. Plan enjoyable activities for the two of you, as well as for the children.

10. Be grateful for the partner you have. Do not attempt to transform him or her into someone else. Instead, look for the excellence in your partner and then appreciate and embrace it. It feels wonderful to cherish someone, and it feels much better to be loved.

Five famous strategies were created by a psychologist named Arthur L. Robin, Ph.D., who has done a study in this area. He is one of the leading specialists on ADHD-affected family structures. He advises optimizing ADHD education and medication. So, the goal is to **change your mindset and develop new abilities.** We will go through each of them to explain them well.

Remember to have fun. It is not just about duties and chores and deadlines and cooling down hot situations; therefore, improving education is important. What exactly do I mean by change your mindset and develop new abilities?

Suppose a person with ADHD goes to the doctor and says, "Excuse me,, my attention drifted. What type of deficiency problem did you refer to?" Sometimes the doctor will provide knowledge, but other times you will not obtain it from her or him.

Books are a good source of information. If you are not a good reader, there are several excellent DVDs and audiotapes available. Support groups are fantastic idea. Seemingly confirming what you thought were your weaknesses, when other people point them out, is a big relief. You may chuckle at this since it's not something you know about you or that's unique to you.

Sometimes, it is good for the partners of adults with ADHD to seek support because you cannot always be there next to your partner. Your constant screaming and venting will not help because they're already on board with the plan to attend therapy and are already struggling to be hopeful about changing their ways of thinking and acting. So, find other people who understand your situation and can validate it. It is really important. You cannot go to a partner with ADHD and say or express everything. Here is what you need to understand ADHD more and be more accommodating of your partner because you have probably tried over-reacting for a few years, and it has not worked that well.

It would help if you first checked the resources. The internet can be a great place to learn about ADHD, especially if you do not live in a big city, but there is a lot of garbage on it. For example, many Scientologists or anti-psychiatry anti-medication people want everyone to believe that every psychiatric diagnosis is a pharmaceutical invention and reading too much can be disheartening.

Work on treatment optimization. What does that imply? It implies you do not just go to the doctor, and he or she offers you some drug and says, "Here, try this." That is not the case. There is a protocol, but you would be surprised how few doctors follow it. It all starts with determining your goals. Where are you finding difficulty? And what, if anything, do you want to improve? Going to bed on time, paying bills, etc. are all things that can be tracked while you start a low dose of medication. You also want to keep a record of irritability, because some medications might make you more irritable and so you should not have to give up "focus" to be more irritable.

There are many medications available, and rather than simply taking whatever the doctor prescribes, you should choose one that works best for you. If you take a medicine, for example at 7:00 a.m., make sure it is active during the frequent sorts of engagement. For most people, it wear off by the time you get home or while you are traveling. Sometimes, when the drug wears off, you experience symptoms that are worse than at the baseline. You get a rebound effect, which by the way is not a good time to be driving. You should ensure that the treating physician has addressed the whole range of symptoms.

If you have coexisting anxiety and depression, address critical things with your partner only while the meds are in effect because, otherwise, you know it will go nowhere. It can quickly devolve into a nasty situation. Once you have found the right prescription and are satisfied with it, adhere to your dosage, which may entail maintaining a record at first because believe it or not, you will forget how things used to be.

I am seeing more folks with ADD saying, "You know, I have been doing fairly well since I have been on this medicine, but I would like to start weaning off it slowly." So, what is the point of doing that? They do not recall what life was like before. Sometimes medicine is required for both partners. It is something you should talk to your doctor about because if you are the partner of an adult with ADHD, you may have developed your psychiatric illness over years, such as depression or anxiety, and if you are a woman, you are especially biologically vulnerable to serotonin loss due to stress. You may need a little boost to get you both over the hump and on the path to improvement and an attitude adjustment.

The adult with ADHD should recognize how the ADHD has impacted their partner. I believe there is a delicate line to cross here. I do not believe in bashing someone over the head if they did something while suffering from an undetected neurocognitive illness. You want to accept responsibility, but I don't think it should hang over someone's head for too long. It is not like they asked for it or wanted it to go unnoticed. It is time to accept responsibility for poor self-regulation acts. This is not to say that you will always be able to mock them; but it does mean you should accept that this happens and agree to stop denying, dismissing, and ignoring the issues.

Nothing can make a spouse angrier and more disgusted than entirely avoiding important matters. Since it has the same emotional impact as hitting somebody in the face. you should become skilled at responding to warnings about poor behavior without becoming defensive. It depends on how it is portrayed. The way criticism is communicated to the ADHD spouse converts blame into empathy.

Remember that if you have one of these extremely ordered prefrontal cortexes, not everyone's brain functions the same way as yours and you may have some concerns such as in the organizing your home. If your ADHD partner prefers visual organizational techniques, you must learn how to make it work for both of you. You may like everything tucked away in a drawer in a filing cabinet. Try to put yourself in your partner's head and experience what it feels like; that only comes from education and knowledge gained from listening to the experts.

It is not that adults with ADHD don't care about themselves, as I've learned so far. Instead, their behaviors are the result of neurological errors rather than hatred or a lack of concern. In fact, I've met a lot of adults with ADHD who work against their own best interests. In other words, it is not personal.

At a meeting I attended, one man showed up. He stated, "I've heard of this oppositional personality trait and I often oppose myself in my own mind." In order for him to fall asleep, he said he must trick himself. If he told himself, "Okay, we're going to bed at ten," his resistance would come to the surface, and he would fight himself. However, he should not do so when lying in bed. In order to fool himself, he will have to say things like, "I'm not going to bed right now, but I'm going into the bedroom and turning on my nightstand lamp." His voice sounds like it is coming from a different speaker.

Just lower the cover if you don't want to go to bed. Right now, I'm not going to sleep. Rather, I'll read in bed. And that's how he gets himself to sleep, he says.

It's always a pleasure to attend my adult ADHD meetings. In our conversations, we gain a great deal of knowledge because many people don't realize they have difficulties until after a few decades. For example, several men in their 40s and 50s understood that their ADHD partner showed trouble accepting responsibility for their actions, but now they know why?

They followed psycho-education and receive tools for change, medication, and other strategies. I cannot tell you how many times I hear this in my partner's group, and I am always stunned by the illogic of it. Many people are overweight, but it doesn't mean they should all consider using an emetic because it's not for everyone. As a matter of fact, it doesn't work that way.

Although becoming aware of the problem is the initial stage of change, it is not the end-all and be-all of the process. You should find a therapist who is highly qualified. If you don't, you'll only exacerbate the problem. Insofar as both couples' viewpoints need to be modified, this becomes a practical matter. Especially in the beginning, both partners are aware that mistakes will be made. As most couples know, this can be a real challenge.

Even without medication or recognizing they have ADD, a person with ADD can do better. It is a roller coaster ride that goes up and then drops down; but after a while, they can't sustain it and become used to it. You're always on the lookout for the other shoe to drop. This means that when you initially begin treatment, you're on alert. But when it drops, it will do so with less force the more you educate yourself and know what you're doing.

After reading this book, you'll be able to forgive each other much more quickly and even laugh at some of your blunders. Tidy up the house, reorganize, develop communication and conflict resolution skills, exercise empathy, compassion, and forgiveness, and ask for help from anybody you can. Those with attention deficit hyperactivity disorder (ADHD) in particular resent outsourcing since they believe it implies they aren't fully qualified. As long as they are doing something, they are not showing weakness. Your plan B will always be available to you, which is a sign of wisdom. However, you should not lose sight of what is most important.

There's no need to wait until the last minute if your companion has ADHD. Afternoon tasks at the office provide a risk that your ADHD partner will be late for a date and different automobiles will be required. Don't sulk and fume while you're waiting to get to the event, then gnaw on your spouse in the car on the way home when he can't escape. When there is a captive audience in the car, make heavy use of humor. Remind yourself to have fun, as it's easy to get caught up in all the tasks that need to be accomplished. For some people, this means planning a date night or something equally foolish.

Keep your focus on the present moment. For their capacity to live in the now, people with ADHD are lauded. When it comes to planning future plans or recalling past events clearly, this is how most people live. ADHD author Emily Chen describes what it means to live in the moment while dealing with ADHD. The excitement can be palpable at times, as these people playfully pounce on their prey while on the prowl.

One thinks themselves to be invincible in those moments as if everything is possible.

This book offers a unique viewpoint on embracing and finding thankfulness in the current moment. How about choosing to be open to whatever happens in the present moment and learning to appreciate it as it happens? Consider letting go of other non-present times with your partner if you don't have ADHD yourself.

This is a way of life we can like. However, if you do not have a solid support system in place, it might be tough to maintain this lifestyle (for example, not paying taxes because you are too busy being in the moment does not work out unless someone else handles it for you...) When an ADHD spouse is "living in the moment" and a non-ADHD spouse is "planning," there can be a lot of friction. The partner who does not have ADHD picks up all the left over material.

On the other hand, based on my experience, there is a lot of potential for compromise too. Many partners do not suffer from attention deficit hyperactivity disorder (ADHD) yet do not spend enough time with their spouses in the present. As a result, people miss innumerable opportunities to enjoy life. ADHD companions can benefit from developing the behaviors necessary to slow down and focus on the past or future when appropriate.

Non-ADHD partners should give themselves the permission and grace to appreciate the present moment more often...to simply accept what is coming at you and "join in on some of the more delightful family lunacy." It's up to you to decide which tasks are allowed to draw you away from the current moment. All of us will feel more at peace if we are able to be aware of the moment at hand.

Of note, empathy and ADHD are two different emotions. It's no secret that people with ADHD have trouble with empathy, which can make interpersonal relationships even more challenging to manage. It would be nice to think that if you were harmed, your partner would be aware of it and try to help you. Many persons with ADHD, on the other hand, find it challenging to maintain connections that last a lifetime.

Any of the following reasons may contribute to a difficulty in comprehending others' emotions:

- ADHD sufferers are thought to have difficulties reading other people's emotional cues, which may cause them to overlook such indications and not react to what the other person wants.
- Distraction is a key component. Despite feeling uneasy and conversing with our husbands, we can still enjoy ourselves, but our husbands can't focus on us for very long. Your partner's empathy will be harder to gauge if you have to remind him to sit still and listen to you.
- A person's gender may have an impact on the outcome. We spend less time now, for example, teaching boys and men how to empathize. Males have not developed the skills of listening and empathizing with women in the same way.
- There is a possibility that neurology will be involved. Those with autism, for example, often have difficulty empathizing with others. Those with attention deficit hyperactivity disorder (ADHD) are also prone to have this problem.
- It could be a result of rage. Couples with ADHD are more likely to display a predisposition toward chronic irritation. In addition, people who are angry are less inclined to sympathize. We lose our ability to empathize when we are defensive. When you are trying to heal the scars left by an ADHD partner's transgressions, they typically go hand in hand. This will make it harder to remain open and empathic if you express hurt.
- Your ADHD spouse's crippling worry and self-doubt may hinder them from moving forward. "This seems like it would be a good place to start. Will I commit a mistake?" There are a lot of male clients who don't know how to help their spouses feel better.
- When someone wants to "fix" your situation rather than listen to you, it can be frustrating. They are indeed trying to help but in an unexpected way.

What can be done about the lack of empathy among people with ADHD? See if you can put these ideas into action:

- Be as clear as possible when stating what you want your partner to pay attention to. the current state of mind, for example, cannot be described by the word "disappointed." As a result, a person with ADHD may feel defensive, believing that your unhappy behavior has something to do with them.
- Try to avoid seeming like you're blaming anyone. Instead of expressing "I feel horrible about COVID and my marriage troubles right now," open the door to empathy by saying, "I am depressed about COVID and how you treated me last night."
- When you need an emotional connection, ask for a hug or a touch in a respectful way. If you have to ask, don't be angry with your partner. This in no way implies that your spouse does not want to help you when he or she is unsure of when you need help. Perhaps they are simply uninformed about the subject.
- Because you never know what will happen in the future, it's important not to make assumptions about how your partner will respond (for all the reasons cited above). If this is not enough, ask for exactly what you need. If you are not interested in solving your spouse's problems, you should let them know right away.
- Discuss emotional issues in non-critical situations for a little bit. Parental issues, COVID, and other topics do not have to be about you. Through practice and experience, you can develop new emotional skills. Do not monopolize the conversation or talk for too long. Let your partner open up to you by giving him or her time to be silent and contemplative instead.

Challenges and Solutions

In our brains, the frontal lobe is responsible for executive functioning. Executive functions are those of the brain that activate, organize, integrate, and manage other functions. It enables people to account for their activities' short- and long-term effects and plan for them. It also allows users to evaluate their efforts in real-time and make required adjustments if such actions are not yielding the expected results.

Russell Barkley, Ph.D., and Tom Brown, Ph.D., are two famous ADHD researchers interested in investigating executive function. Barkley divides executive functions into four categories:

- Working memory that is not vocal
- Speech internalization (verbal working memory)
- Affect/motivation/arousal self-regulation
- Reconstruction (planning and generativity)

Barkley's model is founded on the premise that the inability to self-regulate is at the basis of many of the difficulties that people with ADHD confront. He argues that people with ADHD may be unable to wait for their responses, causing them to behave impulsively and without enough thought of future implications, whether positive or bad.

Brown categorizes executive functions into six distinct "clusters."

- Task organization, prioritization, and activation
- concentrating, maintaining, and transferring attention to a task
- Controlling alertness, maintaining effort, and processing speed
- Managing annoyance and emotion modulation
- Using working memory and retrieving information from memory
- Self-monitoring and self-regulation

According to Brown, these clusters work together, and people with ADHD typically have abnormalities in at least some components of each cluster. Brown feels these deficiencies are clinically connected since they frequently appear together.

Individuals have trouble organizing tasks, getting started, remaining engaged, remaining awake, maintaining a level emotional state, applying working memory and recall, and self-monitoring and controlling actions according to Brown's model, which leads to attentional deficiencies.

Executive function deficits have a negative impact on an individual's capacity to begin, work on, and complete projects. It is also frequently assumed that executive function deficiencies are closely related to ADHD symptoms.

According to one survey done by Dr. Robin who queried 32 couples, each partner came up with a top list of characteristics. Here are the top 10. Get ready for this because sometimes it feels like I am just hitting you on the head ten times.

1. The ADHD partner does not remember being told things
2. Says things without thinking
3. Zones out of the conversation
4. has trouble dealing with frustration
5. Has trouble getting started on a task
6. Underestimates the time needed to complete a task.
7. Leaves a mess after finishing the task
8. Does not finish household projects
9. Does not respond when spoken to while staring at their computer screen
10. Does not plan

From these ten challenges, Dr. Robin narrows down five hot spots:

- Communication
- organization
- managing time
- completing tasks
- eliminating clutter

For the ADD/ADHD spouse, the first thing they can do is join support groups like a DSM-iv group or an ADHD-related one. It is helpful because you find out what other people are doing and can talk with other people who have ADHD. You will find a lot of the same solutions over and over again.

We will talk about how to manage time, how tasks get completed, and then the clutter issue is just a special project. But if you live in a cluttered environment, it is very hard to think straight. I am just giving an outline or basic information on these issues. In the coming chapters, we will discuss each one of them in detail.

Communication

Many partners can deal with some of the neurocognitive slips, some of the forgetting (and whatever), but irritability and miscommunication makes it hard to cope. Good communication can solve many problems, and it starts from good listening. It shows that you care about your partner and value their opinion. Listen first and do not be formulating your response while your partner is talking. You must give it some extra mental effort, which might cost you, but it will be worth it. If you need more time to shape a response, ask for it. Do not feel like you have to process everything and come back with an answer right away because it is often going to be the wrong answer. It is going to get you a bad response. You could say, "Can I think about it a minute" but do not say, "Can I think about it and get back to you in an hour." When you cannot give your partner proper time, it is like showing that your partner does not mean anything to you. In short, never use the words like "later."

Find relaxation techniques to clear your mind. Some couples find it best to go for a walk when they want to talk about something. We see gender differences here, as some men do not do well with soulful exchanges. Where you are staring in each other's eyes, trying to discuss something, it throws them off: it does not work with the male brain. It is better to get the blood moving to the brain by walking and then you are both looking ahead and not looking at each other.

As the partner of the adult with ADHD, try to get your partner's attention before saying something important. Do not just call into the next room with an important piece of news. If they are zoned out, get them back to earth and make eye contact, so you know you have their full attention. Do not discuss issues on the fly as you are going out the door. Sometimes email works best because your partner has a chance to read it and formulate a response and get back to you.

When you want to have a discussion, eliminate all distractions. Turn off the TV, the computer, the kids, and pick a good time. Timing is important but not at the end of a stressful day.

Organization

Try to do the most important things first. This is something that many people with ADD/ADHD forget about because they have their priorities misplaced. So why not break up chores or tasks into smaller chunks of about three or four tasks so do not getting overwhelmed by a giant project, and then have to put it off for another day.

You can add structure through alarms, timers, or bells that go off when it is time to do something scheduled. Also, if something is really important, you should say some motivating words out loud like "you know what I would like to do: I would like to take this out for a ride," or "I will go have fun with this." Pick something that motivates you and something that your spouse would also like to do. Then add action prompts or things that can function s visual reminders such as little notes on the fridge saying "time to call Mom". For the ADD/ADHD spouse, maybe put an urgent reminder on your calendar indicating when you have to go and pick up the kids.

If your ADD/ADHD partner is having a hard time sticking to things, maybe it is about the structure of the project. Ask the spouse if there is a place they prefer to work so you can get them into that environment as much as possible. For example, many people with ADD/ADHD work in spurts. You can set up shop in the kitchen or the office for a while, and then when they get distracted, go to another room where there are fewer distractions.

Organization means sorting at times, so create general folders: one for paperwork instead of having five folders. Do the same with clothing: have everything in one place instead of many different ones because then it is hard to find stuff.

If your spouse with ADHD gets scattered and it is hard for them to stay on task, try asking questions like, what are we doing today? What do we have to get done this week?

Another tip is to start throwing things out if you are looking for something and cannot find it. There may be a drawer full of some old paperwork or even an important document. The best way to find something is to start over with a fresh start. Have your ADHD spouse create a filing system that works for them. It could entail putting things alphabetically or by size - or whatever is best for them to find things more easily.

When it comes to meal planning, you may want to make some lists and shop together. Many people with ADHD are impulsive, so you can help the person stick to their meal planning by going shopping together and sticking to the list. This means having a plan and making sure they do not get distracted.

Also, while you want to try to be proactive about the organization, avoid controlling and micro-managing. People with ADHD need to be organized, but some cannot organize themselves. You can help by buying the folders and boxes for them so they know where things go.

Another tip is to make sure several family members know about their ADHD; you can have them become allies in helping your spouse with their ADD/ADHD. Another suggestion is to have a record keeper or go-to person when something comes up, and maybe have a day planner or organizer.

Managing time

This can be a real challenge for someone with attention deficit who is all over the place, especially when you are a very organized person with everything in its place. It is tough with someone who is very disorganized and has a spouse with ADHD.

The first thing is to try not to get into an argument because they are just busy doing other stuff. The best way to do it is stop being so task-oriented. Instead of getting into a conflict about it, try and make the person see things from your point of view so they know what you are feeling.

There is a nice chart in the book, "Time Management for the ADHD Spouse" by Dr. Robin Vik, showing 50 different ways to work on time management for ADD/ADHD. Pick out the five best for your situation. Do not be afraid to change your options if you are not getting the kind of working-out results.

Resist the urge to do just one more thing before you leave the house: go to bed, leave the office, eat dinner, etc. and that is universal. What happens is you start to think you have a half-hour before you leave, but something in that half-hour turns into three hours because you got involved in a new activity. Other tips: if you are going to be more than ten minutes late, call your partner. Use alarms, automated emails, or whatever you need at the end of the day to help tie up the details and get home.

Workaholics rarely endure for very long since they can burn themselves out at the office. People with ADT or these workaholics keep a clock in front of them. Have you ever seen clocks that indicate physical time? It is red so you can see the passage of time.

So, whatever works for your partner in terms of memory cues, such as sticky notes or a PDA, is fine. Also keep them in one of those small spiral paper notebooks as a reminder. Physical reminders are often very helpful so put notes where you will see them, using different colored markers (or if you are a woman, you could put them in your purse or wallet, or even on the refrigerator). There is also using an appointment book or to-do list unless it is organized; otherwise, it will become just another unopened piece of paper.

Let's say you have a chore for your ADHD partner do. Don't expect them to remember. Instead, print a copy of the chore and put it somewhere where they can see it. Because ADD/ADHD people tend to be impulsive, something will distract them every time. You can help by giving them checklists of what to do throughout their day.

If your spouse is having trouble remembering things, have a post-it note in various areas around the house to remind them. Or you can have a daily schedule where your ADHD partner puts something on it like taking out the trash at 3 pm - or whatever it may be. Also have rewards for doing their tasks so they have more of an incentive to get things done promptly.

Here is another vital hint. Keep a whiteboard handy for messages to your partner and plan a regular time to glance at it, such as once in the morning. Keep communications simple, not a bunch of detailed handwritten and random notes. Make very specific weekend plans, especially if you want to avoid the Saturday morning fight. Have a midweek conversation about your weekend as early as Thursday. Sit down and speak about what you have planned for the weekend because while you want it to be all fun, your partner may think that it is time to replace the bathroom faucets; then and you will disagree and have a fight.

What precisely is the Saturday morning fight syndrome? Some of you may have heard about a specific conflict on Saturday mornings. I discovered a study that shows that kids with ADHD are more stressed on weekends than throughout the week. It is counterintuitive, and I have seen it anecdotally in the adult group because there is no scheduled time when you get up and you know what you are meant to do? You go to school, you go to work, you have a schedule, and the weekend is all unstructured time.

You have a list of things you need to do. Now how do you intend to organize it? How do you manage it? According to one of my clients, "My husband and I used to argue every Saturday morning, and I was not the only one I later discovered." When I questioned the support group, I realized it was because he was setting up conflict and oppositionality, possibly to fuel up his brain." I finally asked, "Do you not understand why we fight every Saturday morning?" He had no idea what he was doing. Yes, he said, but I assumed it was her period.

Do not you believe that something is crystal clear to your ADT partner at the molecular level; it is not always the case? All the husband knew was that he was yelling, with no idea that he was the one responsible for that response.

One bonus tip for people with ADD/ADHD is that sometimes it is okay to ask for help. For example, you can make an appointment ahead of time with a friend or your spouse and have them look over your schedule for the day so that they know what you are up to. This will end up being quite helpful because people forget about things because they are in several different places at one time mentally.

One fact about having a spouse with ADHD is that it takes teamwork, and you both need to work together on this. So, encourage them by seeing how well they can do when they try. Another tip would be if your partner is not motivated. You try stepping in for them. For example, maybe you know you will go clean the kitchen but instead of telling them what you will do, just start cleaning. So, throw out the trash at 3 pm if your spouse with ADHD did not get it done by that time, etc.

Declutter

You can create an environment that will help you stick to your schedule by having everything where you need it at your fingertips and in an order that works for you. The kitchen is the most important place to organize for many people with ADD/ADHD. Some researchers suggest that using technology can help a lot. You can use your computer or an electronic planner, or even alarms. Use the clock on your phone.

Adding structure is important when it comes to time management for ADD/ADHD people. You can start by taking a big pile of papers and separating them into different ones. That takes five minutes, and it is worth it because then when you are trying to find important documents, your bills are in one place instead of all over the desk - or wherever else they might be scattered.

Research shows that many people with ADD/ADHD get distracted. So if you know this is a problem for you personally, try to design your workspace in such a way that it helps you stay on task. For example, some experts suggest shutting the door because sometimes phone ringing or door knocking can throw a wrench into things when you are trying to get something done. Some people even suggest turning off the phone, but you have to decide for yourself whether that is necessary.

Decluttering your surroundings and life is a great challenge for many people with ADHD. The best way to do this is to start small and then work your way up. Set aside 15 minutes or so every day to get rid of things that do not need to be there.

Move away the trash and any unwanted stuff to make life easier. Make sure things do not pile up in the first place. This can be a good incentive for cleaning or organizing because with every trash bag taken out, you can reward the person. Try not to criticize your spouse too much because it will make it harder for them to stick with the decluttering program.

Chapter 8:
Effective Communication Strategies for Adults with ADHD

I t is important to value yourself, not lose yourself or put yourself down. Do not allow others to define you. Validation is understanding how to get your needs fulfilled while being in a relationship. The question is: how can I maintain a good communication style?

In my experience as a professional dealing with ADHD, I can connect with the communication challenges faced by persons with ADHD. The inability to communicate is a major problem for many with ADHD, so let's go over the five-step process for effective communication. In this paradigm, you are in a tough ADHD circumstance where your wounds are being triggered, you are misunderstood, people attribute things to you, or you require assistance. Nonetheless, you do not know how to obtain help because you are embarrassed, ashamed or other people have an unfavorable opinion of you.

Consider the possibility that someone is attempting to place blame on you. It would be preferable if you became aware of it in your mind and had to contend with it. You can accept the truth that you are mistaken, and come to terms with it. "I am confident in my ability to be a nice person." It would be best if you thought out loud in your head. "It was imperative that I reclaim that," ultimately." "I understand that it is not true that I would do something like that."

People assume, rather than verifying, that you are not that kind of person. As a result, you likely had to deal with some of the sentiments of embarrassment or rage that came with being perceived in such a bad light. So let us go over the model so that you may put it to use in any situation that comes your way. There are five steps.

The first two levels are internal; you distinct from your ADD in terms of your core sense of self. Ask: what are some of the negative things I am telling myself? What automatic responses do I have, such as "It is always my fault" or "what is wrong with me"? You needed to distance that from your essential sense of identity. You needed to recall your identity. And it is not the type of person that you are, either. As a result, you needed to get your bearings and distinguish between your basic sense of self and your ADD.

Figuring out what you want or need in a circumstance is the first step. This can be done either emotionally or situationally, depending upon the situation. If you do not know what you require or desire, you will not acquire it. It is unlikely that anyone else will be able to sort it out for you. For example, consider a case in which you need to put in place a different organizational structure. Next, you must understand what it is that makes your brain function properly. You had to figure out what you need to do to work through these feelings, and only after that you should talk.

How to communicate successfully is the goal of the next phase. As a result. Now effective communication comes into play. This is difficult for people because when you feel sorry or wounded, it is difficult to communicate your validation, understanding, and appreciation of the other person, whether for their feelings or viewpoint. You, on the other hand, are feeling vulnerable. As a result, the entire process takes a long time. It is important to indicate that you understand that you are sorry for any discomfort the other person has had, which can be difficult because people with ADHD tend to retreat.

Thoughts are involved in communicating with the other person about what you require or the difficulties you are experiencing, with no intention of putting yourself down or making yourself feel like a loser, such as: "What the hell is wrong with me? Oh, I am sorry, but I cannot seem to get anything right." Instead, describe what happened to you and the kind of scenarios you may encounter that require assistance.

You are the person who is in command. Take command of the situation: simply standing there, distant, or humiliated, is not acceptable. Feel better about yourself, your entire sense of self, and respect yourself while also respecting the other person. That is the purpose of communication. It is not to put yourself down but rather to maintain a positive relationship with the other person. Instead of withdrawing from the situation and ignoring it forever, you must explain what happened. The fact that you care makes a significant difference. You have no notion what is going on in the mind of another individual. The result is that misinterpretation and misinterpretation are very likely to occur.

Going through these phases applies to various situations. You might be distancing yourself from your basic sense of self, determining what you require, and explaining your requirements. Then you pull yourself together, take charge of the situation, and say what you deem appropriate.

The process is straightforward, but not simple to practice because it requires a great deal of effort. It may take a long time to get to a position of acceptance, keep your sense of self, and deal with differences or obstacles. It will require time to become proficient; it will not come naturally. Different things happen all the time at work or in your personal life where you cannot complete the tasks that others have assigned to you. Nobody understands the challenges you are experiencing. "Tell me what to do," you say out loud. "And I am going to do it."

People will assume you are unconcerned about them and their feelings if you do not communicate. As a result, they become offended and retreat, creating a vicious circle.

Impulsiveness is one of the main symptoms of ADHD and it can cause issues well into adulthood. According to a study published in the Journal of the International Neuropsychological Society, "Impulsivity....might be the source of much of the impairment reported in daily life" in people with ADHD. According to the paper, impulsivity comprises three major components: attentional issues, lack of planning, and motor abilities. Oral communication is one area where many adults with ADHD struggle with impulsiveness. You might discover that you:

- Interrupt individuals when they are speaking
- Inappropriate statements or speaking at inopportune times
- monopolize the discussion

- Ignore crucial information of a conversation
- Change the subject of a conversation at random
- Try following strategies for effective communication

Be a good listener!

Speaking clearly and successfully might be difficult for those with ADHD. If this is one of your difficulties, you may have acquired counterproductive communication patterns over time — known as habits — that exacerbate your problems.

For example, if you believe you are being misinterpreted or are not being heard, you may react in two ways. First, you may choose to shut down because you are frustrated or unsure of what to say. Second, you might also "hammer away" and not let the other person speak. Neither of these replies contributes to good communication. These responses may result in even more misunderstandings and even hostility. You can modify if you are prone to either talking too little or too much.

However, before delving into how you might develop new habits, it is critical to recognize that your communication difficulties are not entirely your fault. The other individual could be adding to the misunderstanding. However, because you cannot alter other people, it is easier to concentrate on what you can do to make your conversations more fruitful. Doesn't that make sense?

You might begin by deciding to improve those talents you fall short of. And because some of your communication difficulties are caused by ADHD symptoms, knowing the impact of ADHD is an excellent place to start. Then you can determine which techniques and tools will assist you in becoming more effective communication.

Why do you want to be a good listener?

You already have an intuitive feeling that being a good listener is a positive thing. True. But, if this is a struggle for you right now, you might expect it to take some effort and time to learn how to listen better. So, knowing what is in it for you - the reward — will help motivate you to perform the hard work of improving your listening abilities.

You will be able to do the following if you improve your listening skills:

- Create solid and trusted relationships Others, like you, are more likely to invest in developing relationships when they feel heard.
- Produce better and more appropriate solutions. When you can listen to all stakeholders – family, coworkers, friends, and so on – you can develop clarifications and answers that will work.
- Encourage sincerity and openness. People will be more open to you if they believe they are being heard.
- Feel less worried and more at ease. When you are actively listening, you can concentrate less on figuring out what you want to say.

You think faster than others.

Due to their tendency to think faster than they talk, it can be difficult to hear people with ADHD. According to Professor Ralph G. Nichols, you have more time for tangential ideas since people speak slower than you think. As a result, you may become distracted in your thoughts. Does this sound familiar?

Waiting for the other person to get to their point finally can be virtually unpleasant for ADHD individuals. And then they are lost in contemplation, going from one to the next while losing track of the entire conversation.

They might not understand anything the other person said since they were frustrated quickly and lost their thoughts. So while you will not be able to slow down your thinking, you can learn to listen actively.

How ADHD can make it difficult to listen

Sure, everyone has difficulty listening when someone speaks faster than they think. Your ADHD symptoms, on the other hand, may increase your odds of filling the air with your thoughts. Some of the reasons behind this, as you may already be aware, include challenges:

- External distractions, such as random noises, conversations, phones ringing, and so on, must be avoided.
- Internal distractions, which could include thoughts regarding what the person is saying or completely unrelated ideas, should be avoided.

- Emotions such as irritation, anger, or excitement must be managed.
- retaining an interest in the conversation's subject
- It's ideal if you keep a watch on your actions and don't say anything hastily.

As the "father of listening," Professor Ralph G. Nichol observes, "the use, or misuse, of this extra thought time contains the key to how well a person can concentrate on the spoken word." To improve your ability to focus, pay attention to the numerous contexts you would like to listen to better but have problems actively listening during the following few weeks.

Then practice using the tactics listed below to make the best use of your free time.

#1 Seek to understand

If you have read Stephen Covey's "7 Habits of Highly Effective People," you are familiar with his fifth habit: seek to understand first, then to be understood. Even if you have not heard of it, I am sure you have heard of the concept. However, your ADHD issues mentioned above may make it difficult for you to do so in practice. Even though you probably think it is a wonderful idea in theory,

Because of your ADHD-related issues of poor working memory and emotional regulation, you may be overly focused on getting your point through rather than actively listening. This is especially true for ADHD individuals who feel misunderstood or unheard.

Because you do not have enough place in your working memory at the moment to evaluate both points of view — yours and theirs — your poor working memory may contribute to this propensity. As a result, you concentrate solely on your facts. This concentrated focus could also result from the frustration and/or anger you feel due to your ADHD's difficulties with emotional control.

Understandably, you want to ensure your point is heard. However, if you are not truly listening/understanding the other person's point of view, the conversation will eventually run in circles. And you can grow even more frustrated as a result.

To counteract this possibility, you could take the following steps:

- First, pay attention to their important points – thoughts — and jot them down. Then, do not even try to keep it in your head.
- If you're not sure if you've grasped the main points, ask for a rephrase of what the speaker said.
- Hold off on drawing any conclusions or asking any questions unless you are looking for clarification until you are confident you comprehend the content of what they stated.

The mainline is that you want to ensure that you comprehend the thoughts that the other person is attempting to impart.

#2 Ask detailing questions

You may need to interrupt and offer clarifying questions while trying to understand the other person's viewpoint. This is especially useful when you lose the thread due to internal (thoughts and feelings) or external (distractions). However, you may be hesitant to do so because you are embarrassed to admit that you are not catching everything. I understand. But the more you fill the gap with unrelated thoughts, the more difficult it will be to catch up, right?

To let the other person know you did not grasp everything, use statements like:

"That was a lot of information, and I want to make sure I follow everything."

"Are you saying..."

"I am not sure if I received everything. Could you repeat that?"

I believe you will be surprised to learn that most people will appreciate your attempts to remain engaged in the conversation rather than pretending to listen. I do not know about you, but I can usually sense when someone is not paying attention to what we are saying. So you will, without a doubt, take a mental detour from time to time.

However, if you are willing to ask clarifying questions, you will be able to rejoin the conversation sooner rather than later. There is no harm, no foul.

#3 Be inquisitive.

Curiosity about the other person's thoughts is another method to listen and engage in a conversation actively. This can help to reduce the likelihood of falling down a rabbit hole with your unconnected thoughts. One approach is to try to predict where the conversation will go. Another method would be to look for evidence. For example, examine nonverbal communication (facial expressions, gestures, tone of voice) to evaluate if it adds significance to what is spoken.

#4 It is okay to interrupt once in a while.

Actively listening does not preclude you from sharing your opinions. Sharing your thoughts or observations can be a terrific approach to demonstrate that you are deeply involved. Of course, this is true if your input is valuable and you do not accidentally monopolize the discourse. However, you may be wondering how you can do this if there is no natural gap in the speech. You may also believe that you cannot interrupt because it is impolite to do so. It will take time and practice.

You may, however, learn how to interrupt gracefully. Really. How you interrupt will be determined by the situation. So, if you are chatting to close family or friends, you might not notice and can interject. However, you may find it unpleasant to interrupt other scenarios, such as professional settings or ones where you do not know the people well, especially if the other individual does not appear to welcome your input.

Asking permission is one strategy to utilize when you are unsure if it is appropriate to discuss your opinions. You do not have to worry about being impolite if you do so. Because you are requesting permission before interjecting, you would be shocked by how others react if you have never used this method before. In most circumstances, the other individual will gladly give up the floor. When people believe they have a choice and are not coerced into silence. Of course, you should use terms that feel real to you, but here are a few examples: "Do you mind if I pause for a moment?" "I had an idea about that. Is it okay if I share it?"

#5 Allow yourself enough time to consider

Finally, you may discover that it is advisable to postpone reaching firm conclusions during a conversation if you need time to process, especially if you struggle to digest information. You can also avoid speaking rashly and having regrets later by waiting for your response.

But I understand if you don't want the other person to think you don't have an opinion on this issue. So, to avoid appearing disinterested or perplexed, let them know you need time to mull through your options. Then, of course, if you feel at ease, you might even offer some preliminary remarks. This can be expressed in a variety of ways, including:

"I'm not sure where I'm going to stand on this...what I am thinking right now... But before we make any definitive decisions, I would like to take some time to think about it. When would you be available to meet next week?"

"We have discussed a lot, and I would like to take some time to digest before making any decisions." Is it okay if we meet next Monday to see where we stand?"

"I appreciate the discussion, but I need some time to reflect on it. Do you mind if I respond to you by next Wednesday?"

Of course, you want to express your thoughts. However, you also want to answer in a way that feels natural to you. And in the heat of the moment, you may not always be able to do so.

Key takeaways from listening tips for adults with ADHD

Being an engaged listener can help you in a variety of ways. However, having ADHD can make it difficult to listen well. Conversations may also go awry as a result of your ADHD.

The good thing is that you can make this right. While it will take some time, you can increase your ability to listen actively and participate in conversational exchanges by:

- First and foremost, endeavor to comprehend.
- Enquiring for clarification, being inquisitive when necessary; do interrupt.
- Allowing yourself time to think

People with ADHD need to understand that no matter how well they are dealing with ADHD, there will always be wounds or tender spots that can get you right back to that place. That is why you must recall in your mind repeatedly who you really are? We all are still going through these challenges, too. We are finding ways to cope with it and deal with it even thrive.

It gives people with ADHD a lot of hope that they can get through it too. You must see the whole picture, then you are always going to have difficulties and challenges, but you must move toward your strengths and hold that bigger self-image. Be calm, and just remember to communicate with that good image of yourself in mind. Just do not collapse into this feeling of what is wrong with me, and I have to hide who I am and the self-embrace of who you are.

Practice assertive communication

What exactly is assertive communication? When we communicate assertively, we can express our emotions and needs clearly. More about forceful communication can be found later in this chapter. However, to summarize, if passive communication is like being a doormat and aggressive communication is like treating someone else as if they are also a doormat, assertive communication is like banging on the door.

Just let each other in, but there is one problem: there is only one of them. Affirmative communication is not something that everybody is naturally gifted at: it is a skill that must be learned. It requires time and dedication to master the skill. It is also frightening to ask for what we need. What happens if we are turned down? What happens if the response is, "I do not care what you need"? After all, what if we are not sure what our requirements are?

Here are five ways I have discovered to make the aggressive conversation more manageable:

First and foremost, learn to recognize and name your emotions. Often, when we express our feelings to others, we are making judgments about their actions. For example, I have the impression that you despise me. I am offended and feel insulted. I feel ignored, yet these may be based on feelings on my part. They are not, feelings are internal, and feelings are not external. We are saying that we express our opinions on their behavior, which the other person may completely disagree with.

Because of this, they attempt to dispute or reject, which may be what is happening in Elizabeth's case. Her mother is receptive to hearing what she wants and how she feels, but she becomes frustrated and abruptly terminates the discussion. When Elizabeth speaks, she is expressing her point of view. "When you do not call, I get the impression that you despise me." To be more effective, we must concentrate on our real feelings rather than our thoughts about those sentiments.

If you do not call, it makes me feel worried and alone. If you are not comfortable conversing, it is far more difficult to argue with someone like that. Regarding your emotions, which, let us face it, are valid. The majority of us find it difficult to complete this task. Take shifts with the person who is closest to you. Identifying and naming random feelings. Happy, Enraged, ecstatic. Make use of it. This is the source. You should strive to notice and name your sentiments if you are out of thoughts or bitter, angry, enraged, or impassioned.

Identify your emotions. "When they come up, I get tired with them." "When I practice this workout, I get a rush of excitement." I promise you that it is worthwhile to study, realize, and identify what you require. Because we are often unsure of what our requirements are, this presents a challenge. We might believe that all we require is someone to do the dishes. Rather than this, we need to take on a more equitable share of the responsibilities.

We may believe that we require more texting from someone we are dating. The truth is that what we want is to feel safe in our relationship. As a result, with this advice, practice seeking for the need that lies underneath the necessity. To begin with, then dig a little deeper. What is the purpose of this? If you need to take a day off work because a friend is visiting from out of town. Great. Simply request a day off from work.

In contrast, if you require a day off from work because you are exhausted from working 80-hour weeks, what you require may be a more sustainable work schedule. Addressing this need in one uncomfortable conversation with your manager will help you avoid future stress and burnout. We are not required to share all our information with others. People are often more supportive of our solutions when we get to the root of their problems, which is another advantage of getting to the core of our problems.

Suppose they understand why we require them. We can begin with low-stakes circumstances. Start with safe folks and easy scenarios if you are nervous about learning some form of communication. Inform your best buddy that you have a headache and ask them to turn down the music. You can also request more whipped cream on your coffee from the pleasant server.

This can help you feel more empowered while also improving your communication skills and confidence, which can help you prepare for more tough circumstances in the future. When the stakes are higher or power dynamics at play, such as speaking with your supervisor, it is appropriate to use formal language. If you want to talk about it, be mindful of your body language.

It is not just about the words we choose. It is also reflected in our body language and tone of voice. When we use assertive language while standing over someone seated, it can come out as aggressive to the other person. If we speak hesitantly, we may come across as passive. It is difficult to be taken seriously when we are sobbing or shouting in pain. ADHD can make it difficult to maintain emotional control.

Recognize that our emotions can be extreme and as we become more emotional, our cognitive function begins to deteriorate. So they reach a point where they can no longer make sensible decisions, and it is basically impossible for them to do so after that point. You can simply walk away from a harmful discourse in this situation. At the very least, if they are conscious of their tone of voice, we may adjust it to be more appropriate for the situation.

Furthermore, being aware of our bodies can assist in recognizing when we are beginning to become upset, which can serve as a helpful cue to take a break before we reach that point of no return. Finally, do not put it off any longer. Especially when someone is mistreating or taking advantage of us, we must speak up as soon as possible about bad situations for us before they become a regular occurrence.

For example, I had a wonderful time last week visiting a friend who lives in another nation. The only problem was that she was constantly putting me down in front of others. I did not say anything about it. I reasoned that it did not matter that much after all; and it didn't seem to bother me all that much. It was not a huge deal. However, the difficulty with this was that she was becoming progressively meaner and meaner in her speech.

Since I accepted it and did not call out the harmful behavior, it can continue and get worse. And once something is entrenched in a relationship's dynamic, it is much more difficult to modify it. The same may be said for our requirements. If we develop a connection in which we are always putting the other person's needs, the relationship will not be sustainable, even if the words had a good purpose.

We have the potential of being exploited. Even though it is necessary to consider other people's limitations, it is also important to remember that we all have certain limits of our own. Early in a relationship, if we are clear about what those are, it is much easier to make sure that everyone's needs are met.

We cannot control how individuals react to conflict, and everyone will respond differently. As a result, assertive communication is not a certainty. Nevertheless, we will get what we desire in the end. Of course, we will not always get what we want in healthy relationships, but if we are assertive in our communication regularly, we will get what we need.

How to have important conversation

Sometimes we talk about how to deal with the consequences of a disastrous conversation. Other times, our talk focuses on interactions people are avoiding because they are worried things may go wrong.

These challenges are frequently the result of both a lack of communication skills and ADHD symptoms.

If having challenging talks is difficult for you right now, you have another option. You should be aware when you are about to engage in a critical talk. Stop before your emotions take you down a road you do not want to take. Plan out how to have productive talks.

I will now focus on tactics for noticing and slowing down so you do not say or do something you will later regret.

What are the most important conversations for adults with ADHD?

The first step is to identify the types of talks that may be especially difficult to handle - critical dialogues. They are, according to the writers of Crucial Conversations, discussions between two or more persons in which (1) the stakes are great, (2) opinions differ, and (3) emotions are intense.

I am sure you have been in a lot of discussions where people's points of view differed. Consider your current position. You and your supervisor may differ on how to approach a critical project. Perhaps you and your spouse disagree on how to manage the family funds.

You may also be familiar with conversations in which emotions run high. This is when your rational brain shuts down, and your emotional brain takes over. For example, you may become enraged, terrified, or hurt. Then you either shut down or go on the offensive.

But, when the stakes are great, what does it mean? It is possible that if the project on which you and your boss disagree fails, the company will lose a significant client. And, if you are unable to address this argument, your connection with her may be jeopardized. Maybe indefinitely, right? After all, you never know what the long-term implications of a bad interaction will be.

Similarly, every time you have a bad talk with your partner, it is more difficult to have the next one. And when it comes to finances, another emotionally charged subject, there are many major ramifications if you do not handle them properly.

Knowing how to manage these conversations successfully is advantageous, right?

Why are crucial conversations so difficult for adults with ADHD?

While most of us find it challenging to conduct important tasks successfully, ADHD adults typically find them especially tough. Being aware of your ADHD issues, such as those listed below, can help you understand why this is the case and develop realistic techniques for having healthy discussions.

Working memory issues may make it difficult for you to gather, organize, and process information to participate effectively in a discussion, especially if it is fast-paced.

Because of difficulties with emotional regulation, a conversation may begin pleasantly but quickly deteriorate into a dispute. It's possible that you're feeling overwhelmed by the constant back and forth of conversations, especially if they're "passionate" about it. So, you might find it difficult to focus on all aspects of the topic.

And, if you are feeling overloaded and over-stimulated as a result of the aforementioned ADHD-related issues, important talks may be tough for you.

How to stop leading your actions by your stories

Yes, adults with ADHD struggle with emotional regulation. You know where it may take you if you let your emotions guide your actions. And you may believe that you do not influence how you feel. Perhaps you think that other people are to blame for making you angry, terrified, or hurt.

However, most conversations go sour because of the stories we tell ourselves about the facts. Yet, as we will see below in the instance of Yaiza, it is these stories that might cause us to feel and act in specific ways.

Yaiza and her supervisor, Erica, could not agree on who should speak at the conference their company was organizing. Yaiza, therefore, concluded that Erica did not respect her. She complained to her coworkers Erica never listened to her. This was her tale. And the more she thought about it, the more enraged she felt.

As a result, Yaiza felt it was time to put an end to this "awful treatment." And the only way to accomplish this was for her to express her thoughts to her supervisor. So, in their one-on-one, Yaiza, increasing her voice, informed Erica, "If we have the speakers you want, the conference is going to tank." I am certain of it! You've got no clue what you're doing!"

The chances of having a healthy dialogue have also decreased. Does this sound familiar? The key to avoiding this path is to:

- understand your backstory
- then take a pause
- investigate whether another credible story exists
- and once you have learned how to have effective discussions, put them into practice

However, because emotional regulation is difficult, you may be drawn into the conflict before you have had a chance to explore your experience. The trick to avoiding this is to notice the indicators that indicate you are about to engage in a critical dialogue.

How can you tell if you're having a crucial conversation?

When you notice the indications that a critical conversation is about to begin, you can utilize this information to decide whether to pause. And pausing is essential for not saying or doing anything you will come to regret later.

You can begin by observing your cues, such as: physical cues, such as chest tightness, a racing heart, and so on. Then there are thoughts, cognitive clues, retaliation, putdowns, and more. Don't forget shutting down, retreating, sarcastic, not establishing eye contact, or clenching your fist as examples of actions or behavioral signs. Emotional cues abound such as feeling insulted, embarrassed, rejected, or exhausted may come alongside or beneath your anger.

What are your red flags indicating that you're about to enter into an important conversation?

How to be aware of the conditions of the conversation

Keep an eye on what's going on in the "room." if you want to know if you are starting a critical dialogue. That is, you should be able to comprehend the heat of the movement. Is there dread, rage, submission, or something else?

According to Patterson et al., when this occurs, persons who cannot navigate the conversation may encounter silence or violence. You have seen how this appears. When there is silence, people may shut down or physically leave the room to escape the topic. In other cases, people may shift the subject to exit the conversation. Another method people avoid saying what they mean is by using sarcasm or sugarcoating their remarks.

People that are violent in speech, on the other hand, may try to persuade you into their point of view. They may also label ideas or persons as harmful or incorrect. People may also ridicule or threaten others in severe cases.

Chapter 9:
How to Communicate with a Person with ADHD

T his chapter is primarily directed at people who love someone with ADHD or friends with ADHD. But it might also be useful for people who have ADHD. If you have to communicate with someone who has ADHD either in a work environment or in a personal relationship, you might have noticed that they can be a little bit sensitive, which is funny because they are also really insensitive sometimes. Sometimes, they can be quite rude, they tend to talk a lot, which is funny, because they also interrupt a lot.

Sometimes it can be hard to follow the train of thought of a person with ADHD. All of these issues add up to some friction and communication. It is really important to understand how the ADHD brain works. There are some differences in communication between ADHD people and neurotypical people. This chapter aims to help people who do not have ADHD understand how to communicate smoother with their ADHD friends and loved ones because we all want better communication.

A study done at the University of Waterloo in Canada found that people with ADHD have difficulty speaking and interacting. Their ability to consider the perspectives of others, in particular, is impaired as compared to persons who do not have ADHD. A Psych Central article regarding the study that associated ADHD with communication issues, contained the following: "Discussion requires that participants listen carefully and consider the perspectives of others," stated co-author Professor Elizabeth Nilsen, Ph.D. "The ability to see the other person's point of view is critical for effective communication, allowing each speaker to adjust their response or reaction accordingly."

Researchers studied children with and without a diagnosis of ADHD in one trial, and undergraduate students with varying levels of ADHD symptoms participated in the other. Participants had to follow directions from another person who had an obstructed view of some items to move objects in a display case.

Participants with ADHD made more errors while trying to understand which items they were instructed to move based on their partner's limited view of the objects, according to cameras that caught where the participants were looking as they heard the instructions.

A person's ability to use the speaker's perspective to influence their responses decreases with the increasing severity of ADHD symptoms, according to the research. In other words, ADHD symptoms and communication problems are directly related.

On the other hand, You may have noticed that some people with ADHD are fairly sensitive. This is because an aspect of having ADHD that many people with ADHD have is RSD, rejection sensitivity, and dysphoria. What it means is that even if communication is neutral, a person with RSD might feel there is a critique involved or a rejection or judgment, even if is not based in fact; they are always on the lookout for signs that this is happening in every conversation.

So even something innocent said by a non-ADHD may be taken as judgment and is therefore a disappointment. Mocking RSD can cause a person with ADHD to have a full-blown mood swing; emotional dysregulation is a part of ADHD. In the face of a hurtful offhand comment, a person with ADHD would have a hard time not obsessing over. It is hard to recover from; as a result, you might notice that people with ADHD come across as being overly sensitive, thin-skinned, or really cannot take a joke.

For a person with ADHD, this is something really real, and it is very hard to deal with. It can take up a lot of time and emotional energy to manage the feeling of rejection all the time. What do I mean when I talk about emotional regulation? People with ADHD tend to feel very big emotions; they are sometimes very quick to experience very deep feelings when they get sad.

On the other hand, they get really up when happy. In short, they can be very quick to change moods. Emotional regulation is when the brain can handle emotional reactions to various stimuli. So if something mildly annoying happens, it should not ruin your entire day or even your week. But for a person with ADHD, that might be the case because the response does not match the precipitating factor. If you think about it, a person with ADHD has a big job on their hands when they are learning to manage their own emotions, which do not always match the situation.

So on the flip side of this, people with ADHD can sometimes be insensitive and downright rude. The thing is, people with ADHD are often firing on mental overload. So even though they are having a conversation with you, three, four, or five different things are going on in their heads. It is like being in a noisy sports bar with all the different TVs turned to different channel at once.

It is often the case that a person with ADHD may not even notice what they said. Or they may have been talking so quickly and expressing their ideas so fast that they did not stop to analyze whether what they said was appropriate or not.

They think as they are talking instead of thinking, then filtering whether it is appropriate to say it and then it is said, without a filter. Obviously, some things are inappropriate, rude, or weird, and the person with ADHD may not even notice. However, chances are if they do notice it, it makes their RSD a whole lot worse. "Oh, what did I say? Why do I say that? I am so dumb. Oh my god, they hate me. I am so embarrassed. I cannot go back to school again. Why do I do that?"

The other thing about having ADHD is that you have so much going on so fast, and your ability to regulate your attention where it needs to go is not working. Sometimes, people with ADHD can be in a bad mood or not feeling well without noticing it. So, if something happens and you feel tense, your shoulders are scrunch up and your jaws clench. But you do not notice that your back is sore because you are so caught up in what is going on around you.

Then maybe you have not eaten all day and any water to drink. Physiologically, you might be in a really bad place, but you do not even notice the brain-body disconnect. A person with ADHD might be more crabby than they realize and not be able to manage they situations they put themselves in.

If a person with ADHD is looking at his/her phone or typing on a computer, it might look like they are doing something rather unimportant. But what you cannot see is that they are using all their focus at that moment: all their power is going to paying attention to one thing. When somebody asks them an offhand question ("Hey, want a cup of coffee"), it is like a giant train just came crashing into the station and derailed all the train cars. They might bite the person's head off and yell, "Oh, why do not you talk to me later, blah, blah, blah" because you really cannot see how much mental energy and focus it takes for them to be working on their tasks. It is a Herculean effort for people with ADHD to pay attention to one thing, and they may not have the language to explain what they need in terms of boundaries - like just being left alone when working.

So, part of the issue with ADHD is distractibility. You may find that when you talk with a friend who has ADHD, they do not even finish one thought before they are on to the next one. One thought is quickly followed by another. Because of verbal processing, as they are talking, it reminds them of something they forgot. And that reminds them of something else that they had forgotten. This can make it hard to have a meaningful conversation.

When one person talks in a continuous stream without giving the other a chance to talk, it does not make sense because they are not getting anywhere. The flip side is that people with ADHD can interrupt a lot. This has to do a lot with their impulsiveness. The part of the brain that regulates impulsivity in people with ADHD is under-functioning. That is why people with ADHD generally take stimulant medication. They have much energy already, but the stimulation goes to the part of their prefrontal cortex that needs more control. This increases brain activity in this particular area, and then that part of the brain can control their impulsiveness. Sometimes, however, an action may be taken before the person's brain can catch up.

ADD/ADHD patients have a Ferrari-like brain with a bicycle brake. So the brakes do not match the engine, and they cannot slow it down. Interrupting is rude and disruptive to a conversation or meeting. But it is not always something that the person with ADHD is even trying to do. It happens without them meaning to do it.

Now we have a better understanding of some of the challenges associated with interacting with someone who has ADHD. But how can we resolve it and make it better? I will give you ten tips and tricks that I came up with to help you navigate communication with your person who has ADHD, and, hopefully, you will along with them a little better. Not every person with ADHD is the same. Even though they have commonalities in their brain wiring, they all have different personalities, and they come from different cultures and backgrounds. So take each tip with a grain of salt and use what works for you.

Front-loading information means that you tell the person upfront the things that will happen or even the conclusion of the conversation with no surprises. "Hey, Bill, today we are having a meeting. I am going to need you to make sure that you can come on time and take notes as well. A person is coming to the meeting who will be talking to us about a project next week. That is important. So, while you are at the meeting, try to start thinking about ways to contribute to this project."

It is better than, "Hey, Bill, this guy is coming to a meeting today and it is important and then at the meeting when Bill shows up without his notebook. He does not know how he is supposed to participate, being disappointed in him or being frustrated."

Another example might be, "Hey, honey, we need to get ready to leave for my mom and dad's Christmas party in about an hour. I need to stop at the post office; however, could you do me a favor? When we are in the car, can you sit in the back with the baby and like not use your phone to play games, but like, hang out with her because sometimes she gets upset when I get out of the car," as opposed to "Hey, honey, be for the Christmas party in 20 minutes. Get off your phone, I am going to the post office so hang out with the baby while I am there".

Front-loading information gives people with ADHD a chance to understand the steps because their sense of time is now. Knowing what we will need from them takes all the guesswork out of it. It also means that at that moment, they will not come ill-prepared. They have support in being prepared. So, front-loading information allows them to be prepared.

Front-loading is more a direct request to avoid distractions. They do have the ability to pay attention, but they do not always know when they are going to need it. And they do not have a lot of it, so it is good to let them know when you need it. This is also a good strategy to use with people who have ADHD who tend to hyper-focus because if they are fixated on something, it can be really hard to transition away from what they are doing.

If you have something important to say , you need someone's attention, or you need them to remember something, it is a good idea to prep and prime them for shifting their attention. Sometimes this is a very manual task for them.

"Hey, Adam, I have something I need to talk to you about that is important. So when you are done what you are doing, can you come and talk about it?"

"Hey, there, baby! Want to discuss something of great importance. And I would like for you to listen until I am done talking and not interrupt. If you have thoughts and feelings about what I am saying, I want to hear them. And I am going to make sure to make space for you to listen to me. But I need to talk through this with and let you know what is going on. So please listen, do not interrupt, and then let me know what you think afterward, okay."

People with ADHD do not generally like being talked down to as if they are children. But unfortunately because they are forgetful, they get interrupted. After all, their behavior might be childish at times. It happens a lot. Research has found that people with ADHD are about 30% behind in development compared to their peers. So a person in their early 20s might act and behave more like someone in their late teens, someone who is 14 might be more like a 10-year-old, and so forth. However, despite this, many people with ADHD are very intelligent. They know when they are being talked down to. They are not idiots.

Combine that with the rejection sensitivity dysphoria and it exacerbates the problem. Talking down to a person with ADHD is fairly unwelcome and will result in a negative interaction. It does not mean that you cannot hold someone with ADHD responsible for their bad behavior;

instead of talking down to them, without judgment or condescension remind them of what the rules are.

You have likely addressed recurrent issues and made some rules around them. Do not expect the person with ADHD to remember them automatically; they probably will start to remember them after a while. Just dispassionately remind them not to take it personally and do not make a big deal out of it.

"Remember that we made a rule about not talking about finances when we have been drinking? We both had a couple of beers. So can we maybe talk about something else? I do not want us to get into a fight."

"Tell me about how it was when you went to the auto repair shop. I hear that you are frustrated about what is going on with the car. You must be feeling passionate about getting it fixed. But what you just said hurt my feelings. There are certain problems with our car that I want to discuss. But if you are going to be insulting and not be able without raising your voice, maybe we should not talk about it right now. So, do you want to hear about what the mechanic said? Okay, so you are still raising your voice. I can see that this has got you emotional. That is fine. Let us talk about it another time."

We know that people with ADHD can sometimes take things personally or be sensitive to feedback and critiques. But it does not mean that people with ADHD get a free pass not to be held accountable. It is good to remind them that they want to be held accountable and acknowledge the things they did. With rejection sensitivity, it can make them feel like they are the worst person in the world.

Because of the way the ADHD brain is wired, they often only see the worst in themselves. So when someone is trying to tell them something they did wrong, it can be really hard to listen without justifying all the other things that they did. It can make the person giving the critique feel like they are not being listened to or the issue is not being acknowledged.

A really good way to combat this is to give a bit of verbal acknowledgment of what was done right. This will put the person with ADHD at ease because it will help them know that you do not only see the bad things about them. Number two, you are not coming from a place of judgment, but you genuinely want them to work on the issue. It will help them feel validated as a person and appreciated for the work they have already done - whatever that may be. Sometimes it is so hard to do things right when you have ADHD. It can feel super hurtful and hard to listen when people only focus on what you did wrong.

"Hey, Frank, I love that you took the initiative to make dinner; it was so good. That was fun to have you cook. But the kitchen is a huge mess. And so you know, I would love it. So if you would cook again, that was super awesome. But next time, can you maybe clean up a little more as you go. And then I can help out by doing the dishes afterward. Because just like it is crazy in there."

"Hey, Ashley, great job stocking the beer fridge; you were so fast. I am impressed by how quickly you have got everything stocked in there. Just one thing, however. A couple of these beers are actually in the wrong place. I need you to go back and switch them. There are about three of them. That was amazing how quickly you did that; I will get you to do that more in the future. Good job."

The love buffer is more of a general verbal acknowledgment. If a person with ADHD is behaving badly, you need to have some difficult dialogue. It is less about acknowledging the specific good things they do or something bad; you need them to change. Just letting them know that they are cared about loved will make them receptive to hearing about the issues.

The ultimate goal of a conversation like this is to have the person with ADHD listen to you and be open and vulnerable. They should not get caught up in their rejection sensitivity, dysphoria, and feel the need to start explaining and being defensive. When that happens, you are not making them feel heard and loved and cared about. They are also emotionally dysregulated. So it is upsetting for both parties when you need to talk about something important.

The person with ADHD makes it all about them and their hurt feelings, and they cannot listen. They are defensive, and ultimately if they are your partner, a family member, or somebody important in your life, they want you to make them feel cared about. This allows the person with ADHD to give you what you need.

"Hey, Jenny, thanks for coming to this meeting with me. First of all, I just wanted to start by saying you are doing an awesome job. You are an awesome supervisor, and you are fast at doing the cash; the customers all loves you. I am impressed with you. There is one thing I need you to work on, however. It is the way you communicate with the other employees. As a supervisor, you to start being a little more careful with the language you use and make sure you are appropriate. That will help to make the team feel a bit more supported by you. You have done a great job here, and I appreciate it greatly. So can you work on improving that? Okay, thank you".

"Honey, I need to talk to you about something really serious. But before I do that, let me tell you that I love you so much. No matter what happens, we are always going to be together. I am here for you and I support you. But when you go out with your friends on Friday night, you come home really, really drunk. You're noisy, and it's been difficult for me. You are frankly obnoxious and make a big mess. You do not clean up after yourself. So this drinking on Fridays is a problem for me. Okay."

Some people are verbal processors. If you have a verbal processor in your life, you what it is like: they talk in a steady stream without stopping, and you cannot get a word in edgewise. They will go from topic to topic to topic; you can almost see their thoughts wandering. It can be challenging, especially if you work with a person like that when meetings are time-sensitive. Often, a verbally processing person may not even realize it because they think their thoughts as they are saying them. They are not doing it on purpose. Although people with ADHD are sensitive creatures, they do not mind being brought back to the straight path gently. Tell them to get to the point.

"I am so sorry to interrupt you. But I do not understand what you are telling me. Can you bottom line this information for me? When is the date for the event going to happen?"

OR

"Darrell, Darrell, I am so sorry to interrupt you as this seems interesting. I have to be incredibly cautious of the time I'm spending. I have only got about two minutes before I have to go pick up my son from daycare. So can you just let me know, like, what are the things that you need for me to be ready for the party?"

OR

"That sounds like such an awesome. Thanks for letting me know you had a fantastic time at Disneyland! And I would love to hear more about it later. But I got to run. Okay, so you need paper plates. You need balloons. Okay, cool. Yeah, I can do that. Thank you so much."

Setting boundaries

People with ADHD tend to have trouble setting and maintaining boundaries and struggle to respect them, partially because they struggle to remember them. If you have a person in your life with ADHD, you probably have noticed that they are not great with boundaries. This is a challenge because when they do not know their boundaries, it will often lead to them snapping at you. After all, you have maybe crossed a boundary and do not even realize it. What you can do for your beloved with ADHD is help them learn how to set better boundaries by modeling good behavior.

It is in your best interest to learn about setting and communicating healthy boundaries, not just for better interactions with your ADHD person, but also for yourself. Healthy boundaries are good for all of us. A healthy boundary is not punishing or lashing out at someone for doing something you do not like or is inappropriate. In order to keep ourselves secure and protected from situations that are not acceptable, we must set boundaries.

A really good example might be: whenever I speak to my friend, Paul, he starts talking about politics. He has a different political outlook than me and things get really heated. I get really upset. So my boundary with Paul is this, I cannot talk politics with him now. Can I control what Paul talks about? Not all the time? But I can ask him politely not to talk to me about politics and to be aware that politics is a sore subject. Does Paul have to do what I ask him? No, absolutely not. But I am Paul's friend. He cares about me and wants to make sure I am comfortable.

So, I can negotiate with Paul over what the boundary looks like. What do I do if Paul does not respect my boundaries. If you have a person with ADHD in your life, you are probably going to have to remind them, and that does not mean lashing out at them. It just means being assertive. "Paul, sorry, I have already talked about this. Let's not talk about politics because, honestly, this is just not okay. Can you please change the subject?" What if Paul does not want to change the subject? Or what if he becomes belligerent? How do I enforce my boundary? I do something to keep myself safe but that does not include yelling at Paul, freaking out, and hammering on - like bah, bah, bah. I might leave the situation, I might hang up the phone, I might go or otherwise disengage from the conversation. Whatever the outcome of enforcing your boundaries, it is essential to take away the risk of getting hurt or in a situation that is uncomfortable.

Enforcing your boundaries with a person with ADHD might look like, "Hey, Ashley, it is so nice to see you. I wish you would call before you come over. I am not able to hang out right now. I have asked you to get in touch with me before you are going to come over. It is not that I do not want to see you, but I am just so busy. I really cannot have this kind of drop-in happening. I just want to remind you. I want to hang out with you, but call before you come over. Like, give me a heads up. Make sure that I am available. Okay? Look, why don't we set another time to hang out soon? But I cannot hang out now, sorry."

OR

"Here is the thing. I have noticed that when you talk about your ex-partner, Anna, you like to get worked up, and often that leads to us fighting. I really do not want to fight with you. So can you not talk about Anna? Maybe talk with your other friends about her. But, honestly, that is not a conversation we can have. That is not a topic that is safe for us to talk about."

OR

"Hey, john. No talking about Anna, okay. I just cannot handle it. Please stop bringing up Anna, or I will have to end the conversation. I do not want to hear about your life with her. I do not want to hear about all the terrible things she did to you. It needs to stop.

OR

"Look, you need to get this stuff off your chest, but I will stop you right here. I am walking away from you right now. I love you. I will talk to you when you want to talk about something else. Have a good day."

Try to have healthy boundaries and stand up for yourself.

Nagging

People with ADHD hate to be nagged. And it is really hard to resist the urge not to do it when their lives are a hot mess. They are probably already trying to engage in one or several systems of managing themselves, remembering to do things in a timely manner.

They know they are a hot mess, and they are working on it. Just because you cannot see it does not mean they are not working on it. So nagging persons with ADHD is unhelpful.

"Do not forget to do this. Did you remember to do that?"

Nagging is bound to get your head bitten off. So what are better question-based reminders? It is like coaching? For example, if you tell me that they have six things to do, instead of saying, "Hey, do not forget to do this. Do not forget to do that. Did you do this yet? "

Say, "Hey, how is your day going? Are you able to make it to the grocery store?

OR

"How is your day going? And how many of those six things that you told me you needed to do earlier? Did you get it done?"

Just ask in order to engage. Help the person process. Help them think; do not just tell them what to do. Nobody likes being told what to do, especially people with ADHD who running out of their battery charge and moving on fast.

Ask them

Ask them how they want to be helped. Do not just assume that they need help. Do not just assume that the best way to help them is by telling them what to do. Don't try to boss them around. Everybody with ADHD has had this experience where they try to explain what is going on with them, and they get an endless laundry list of advice.

"Yes, I have thought of trying to keep track of where I put my keys. Yes, I have thought of trying to use the scheduler. Yes, I have thought of cleaning up before bed. Yes, I have thought of making a budget. Yeah, I tried that." It is more supportive to ask your ADHD person how they want to be helped.

"Hey, Bob, I hear that you are stressed out right now. Is there anything I can do to help? What could I do to help you? Would it help if I give you a reminder of this? Is there some way that I can help you stay on track with this? "

As open-ended questions; maybe the person with ADHD does not want your help. There's nothing quite as irritating as watching someone try to juggle and drop a few balls. You cannot do it for them if they are not open to it. You can lead a horse to water, but you cannot make it drink. Ask them how best you can help, if at all. Please put them in the driver's seat.

Respect that the person with ADHD knows their life and their situation the best and if you love them and want to help this amazing person, let them tell you what they need. Then follow through on it.

It could be that all they need is for you to call them and say, "Hey, did you eat lunch today?" You do not need to assume that you should bring them lunch every day. Just give them a call, "Hey, do you eat lunch today?" Maybe that is all they need.

Finally, know when not to engage them. Understand when not to disturb a person with ADHD. Sometimes they have so much going on and are suffocating under their mind's burden. Just managing their thoughts is a challenge. Managing their emotions is a challenge too. If it does not seem like a good time, try again later.

Sometimes you call, and they put you on hold ("Your call will be answered in like 30 minutes...) You call back another time, but there are too many calls in the queue: you have to come back later. If the person is overly emotional, if they are not respectful, if they are snapping at you, and if they seem overwhelmed, they will not remember what you are asking.

If they start shouting or verbally processing like crazy, it is simply better to know when to walk away and try again at another time. This goes back to boundaries. It is about keeping yourself safe too while doing the best you can for the person you love with ADHD. If you work with them, maybe there are some things that you must talk about or deal with. But unless the building is on fire, it usually can wait, even 30 minutes.

"Hey, I see that this is not a good time. I am going to email you about this."

OR

"Hey, I know this is not a great time; here is a post-it note about the thing that I need. "

The goal is not to have things the way you want them or have the person with ADHD communicate the way you need, but to have the best possible outcome.

Chapter 10:
Time Management for Persons with ADHD

T his chapter will discuss how ADHD affects decision-making, planning, basic abilities, time management, and other duties and responsibilities. When it comes to non-medication methods of managing ADHD symptoms, we can divide it into three categories: time management, organization, and planning. People with ADHD often have difficulty anticipating how long tasks will take and altering their schedules.

Accordingly and as a result, you may be regularly late to activities or may even be unable to complete tasks since you do not consider how long things should take. Also, as a cumulative result of ADHD, you can lose time to activities that you cannot even track. So the first step in mastering the time management skill is to have access to time at all times.

Do you wear a watch? You may claim that you do not need a watch since you have your phone, but you cannot always pull your phone out to check the time. time is continually in your face, so you want your awareness to have a smooth flow. If knowing the time requires too much work, you will probably act without knowing it, believing that you are fine.

You want a watch on your wrist and wall clocks in the rooms where most of your time is spent, such as the kitchen, bedroom, home office, and bathroom. When you are in situations where there is no clock in an easy view, a watch allows you access.

Maybe you do not want to raise your wrist obviously. Have you ever been late for an appointment because you took a 30-minute shower when you thought it would only take five minutes? That is where a bathroom clock comes in handy. The next stage is to estimate how long it takes to do your normal duties. Knowing how long things take will help you plan your day. You want to leave your house on time, knowing how much you can complete before leaving.

A delay might occur due to being distracted, but it can also result from starting something that will take you more time than you have available. Repeatedly leaving things undone erodes motivation and self-esteem. On the other hand, it is very pleasant to finish something, even if it is a minor effort.

You want to construct a list of your normal tasks and over a few days you will know how long it takes you. take, preparing for school or work. If this activity takes you more than an hour, you should divide it into subtasks to identify what takes the longest and keep that part separate.

Showering and grooming yourself may take 40 minutes. Next, brush your teeth, comb your hair, and so on. Then divide your time between eating, making your lunch, and getting out of bed. Then add things like laundry, dishes, other housework, walking your dog, and sorting your mail. Finally, assume you have a task that you never seem to do in one sitting.

As a result, you are always behind because incomplete work piles up. You can use this exercise to schedule the activity and split it down into phases. Now you can watch how time passes. Here is an illustration. Judy becomes nervous when she thinks about the mountains of laundry she cannot keep under control.

She first calculated that it would take her around two hours to complete the wash and dry cycles, followed by another 30 minutes to fold. However, she always has piles of clean clothes in baskets and a bed in the guest room. The family enters the room to retrieve clothing off the bed. As a result, clothes tumble to the floor and are stepped on, making it impossible to detect what is clean and what is not.

You wonder why others cannot fold their clothing. But it is not the point. The key point is in her mind: Judy considers laundry to be the simple act of placing clothes in a washing machine. It only takes approximately two and a half hours, but she cannot find a two and a half-hour block of time.

To complete this activity successfully, it was necessary to separate the many components of doing laundry and know how much time was required to perform each of those tasks. When Judy did that, she noticed that it took her 15 minutes to gather all of the clothes from everyone's room, transport them downstairs, and load them into the washing machine.

The wash and dryer cycles took an hour and a half to complete. Folding the clothes took anything from 10 to 20 minutes, and putting them away took another 10 minutes. So, Judy spends the first 15 minutes gathering the laundry. After an hour and a half break, each will take another 30 minutes to process.

Every week, she did four to five loads of laundry with her family. So understanding that folding and putting away clothing could easily take a couple of hours helped Judy plan how she did the laundry because one of her concerns was that she set an unrealistic goal for herself to do laundry every day.

It was overwhelming because there were so many steps, and she could not keep her mind on the final one. This is especially difficult when the next stage requires you to wait an hour and a half. As a result, the natural tendency would be to put it off till later. However, knowing that the second section of the washing would take a couple of hours allowed Judy to schedule it separately and then break it down into steps.

Once she is finished with the mountain of laundry on her bed, she will set aside time to sort, fold, and put away. This may appear to be common sense. And if it does, it is most likely because you do not have this condition, but ADHD creates issues with executive functioning, which involves time management, estimate, and organizing.

When you are faced with a task that involves numerous steps, it is all too easy to lose track and have them drop off or be left undone in a way that causes complications. For example, not knowing where your clothes are because they are hidden beneath a mound, or your favorite items have slipped under the bed after someone has walked over them.

This means that finding things to wear can take an extra 20 minutes in the morning. The problem with time is that it has a cascading impact. This brings up a point: if you were timing your morning activities, you might want to include how much time you spend looking for clothes as well.

The time awareness exercise can be divided into two halves. The first step is to estimate how long it will take to complete your typical duties. It's not a situation you want to take chances with. You should look at your watch and record the start and end times in a time log. The second step is to think about what makes it a long time to do something and cause you to be late. Break it down into smaller jobs and then time them.

This time log can be used afterward to organize your day and address issues that are taking up too much of your time. For example, suppose you spend 15 minutes each morning deciding what to wear or looking for clothes. As a result, you can utilize this list to save time.

Planners

The third and final step I will discuss is keeping a planner. I recommend two types: a daily planner for keeping track of your daily activities and a weekly at-a-glance calendar for a bird's eye view of what is going on in your life and what is new in the field.

You'll want to carry it around with you at all times. It does not have to be made of paper. It might be done digitally. With ADHD, if you are more comfortable utilizing something on your phone, out of sight is out of mind. As a result, if it is not on your calendar, it does not exist. You do not want to clog your head with all of the things you need to remember to do; if you recall well, that is fantastic, but you do not want the weight of trying to remember since with ADHD, mental clutter is cleansed without your knowledge. In fact, your brain lets go of it for you.

Then the information has vanished until you are reminded of what you meant. For example, you want to add appointments and tasks to your planner now that you know how long things will take. You should consult your planner at the start and end of the day; consult it at the beginning of the day to obtain an overview of what you have to complete for the day.

Then you will want to look at it at the end of the day to see what was left undone and what you have planned for the next day. If there are any tasks you did not complete, you should reschedule them. It could be the next day or several days later.

If you observe a trend of specific things you never manage to do when you thought you should, it can be a task to break down into subtasks and put on your to-do list as separate items. Getting all this going may appear to be a lot of labor when things seem daunting to begin with. It indicates that the task is too large. So divide it into halves. To recap, begin by acquiring a watch and a sufficient number of visible clocks in areas where you spend time and then make your time log, using your wristwatches and clocks.

This could take several days. Begin with the main things such as getting ready for work, doing chores, eating dinner, and getting ready for bed. Your list can include things you do at work as well so you can better understand how you spend your time at work. And this is to teach you to value time.

Finally, you will be given a daily plan. In addition a weekly or monthly planner, you will utilize the daily planner to keep track of your appointments, obligations, and to-do list. And you will consult the planner twice a day: once in the morning to assess the extent of your day and once in the evening to reflect on how your day went and assess what you have planned for the next day. It allows you to reschedule tasks that you did not accomplish.

Procrastination

With attention deficit hyperactivity disorder, procrastination is a major issue. Of course, nobody wants to do unpleasant things, but if you have

ADHD, you can avoid doing something simply because the breadth of the activity appears to be too great. It may have too many stages, or you believe it will take too long. In cognitive behavior therapy, these are referred to as unpleasant tasks, as they appear to be too painful to begin or finish. That's one of the most typical causes for their avoidance. After that, it is about being monotonous and routine. If it is dull and takes too long, you lose interest.

Watching something on television, going on a walk with a group, conversing with friends, or listening to a fascinating podcast episode are all instances of pleasant tasks. However, you do not want it to be something to eat, such as a piece of cake because you do not want to associate the reward with eating, which reinforces emotions.

It is advisable to make a list of rewarding tasks to keep on hand so you can quickly choose from the list when you are presented with something you do not want to do. Include the time it takes to complete the reward. You find it rewarding if you cannot think of anything else to do.

Consider what you would rather do instead of an unpleasant. It has to be something you would do if you were in your right mind. Unfortunately, that is not always the case. You would rather be in Bali, thinking, "I do not feel like doing this. I will watch an episode of Westworld." Then, as a reward, you will be motivated to complete the assignment.

So, you power through the work to get to the rubric. I have already discussed how to keep a time diary of how long things take and how to schedule tasks in your planner. If you include a reward at the end of a task, make sure to include it in your time log. You could also employ regularly scheduled enjoyable activities as a motivator.

This means you would plan your unpleasant activity around natural breaks. For example, assume you regularly watch the news at a specific hour and enjoy doing so. Then prepare to conduct your hour-long unpleasant task one hour before the news show; then you may recover by watching the news.

Another technique to employ the reward system is to undertake the pleasure activity while doing the painful one. So, with this technique, you would consult your planner to determine what you needed to complete that day. And then there are things you can pair with something fun, such as doing laundry while watching TV or listening to a podcast episode while exercising.

Imagine you do not want to do anything else while performing the task because it requires a lot of concentration or focus. Find a way to do the activity in a relaxing environment. For example, instead of sitting at a computer to make an online insurance claim, do it away your deck or in a comfortable chair.

Comfortable settings help mitigate the terrible feeling of having to accomplish a chore. It is not something you would think to do. You must intend to complete the painful task in a nice setting. You may get it done if you push through, but you reinforce the experience as something truly unplug.

And if you have to do it again, it may be more difficult to push through the second time because you remember how much you disliked doing it the first time. So you are attempting to make yourself dislike it less using this method. As a result, there will be less reluctance to do the next time. Prioritizing the tasks on your to-do list is another method for getting things done.

Stephen Kobe authored the book "The Seven Habits of Highly Effective People." In the book, he suggests prioritizing chores based on their level of urgency and relevance. Using this method, you may categorize your priorities as important and urgent, important but not urgent, important but not urgent, important but not urgent, important but not urgent, and not.

Regardless of their relevance, urgent things tend to drive us more, and things can become urgent merely because they were postponed for a later time. As a result, they wind up taking precedence over something that could have been more necessary but was not urgently important, such as those required for your job or education.

They are urgent because the deadlines are set in stone. Important but not urgent things could include exercising, going food shopping so you can prepare a healthy meal instead of ordering takeout, and not important. Still, critical things could consist of things that do not necessarily have much relevance to you but are made urgent by someone else's impatience.

Perhaps someone asks you to do something, but they require it immediately because they waited until the last minute. If you want to be a team player or support them, you will meet their timeline, and then not important and not urgent tend to be pipe dreams, something you would like to do at some point, like reorganize your closet, or something someone else could do for you.

And these are usually appealing in some way, either because they do not demand a lot of thought or they are enjoyable. And if that is the case, this would be something you would do in your spare time. Because these undertakings are appealing, it may become a weekend project.

It is easy to be pulled to and think of them as more essential than they are since they provide a positive result. "It feels great to get rid of things in my closet that I do not need. As a result, I ask tell myself, is it vital?"

How to do those activities that you might otherwise put off? Pairing enjoyable activities with unpleasant ones are one of the two best tips. Of course, this means you have already created a work list and determined which sections are undesirable as well as how long it should take.

You can also create a cozy setting to conduct the unpleasant activity, such as taking nasty tasting medicine with something sweet, and you can change the time you do the disliked activities just before you do something you enjoy.

The second piece of advice for completing chores on time is to prioritize them in order of importance. This helps prevent wasting time on insignificant things so that everything vital does not become urgent; fire drills beget additional fire drills and a perpetual state of urgency. And playing catch-up requires a lot of energy and makes you disregard crucial things.

Chapter 11:
Getting Things Done

L et's have a look at a well-known book, "Getting Things Done" by David Allen, which I often recommend to my clients although it can be difficult to get through. I am hoping that I can condense the key elements down to something that readers can digest.

This amazing book it can be a little bit over the top for people with ADHD. The gist of it is that people with ADHD should get everything out of their heads and put it into a system they trust. There is no "Oh, I forgot to take care of whatever." And then they run and take care of whatever. And then, "I am going to do this," and then an hour later they realize, "Oh, I had never done this critical thing that I had to do in time."

People with ADHD should get everything out of their heads. It frees up the mental bandwidth for doing other things. It is a bit different than just a to-do list: it is a complete system. According to David Allen, it comes down to the tool they use. It could be paper o ra phone app. It should be what I call a master list of everything they have to do.

When I introduce this idea of a master list, I usually find that people are like, "oh no, that is too overwhelming. I cannot possibly do that". That is where another very important principle of getting things done comes in. How will people with ADHD manage the list? It is a very important step. So when they have everything out of their heads, they can figure out, for each thing, "is this something I am going to do? Is it something I am going to delegate? Is it something I am going to defer? Is it something that I can drop?" People with ADHD review the essential things in their trusted system and what are they going to do today?

People with ADHD manage these things by priority. First they figure out, roughly, what are they going to do, or the most important task so that they do not have a massive database of stuff to take care of. The first step is the collection process of gathering everything together. It could be digital stuff (software or an email inbox) and/or physical stuff (a cardboard box). All physical things go into one inbox, and all emails, etc. go in the digital collection box.

Each item represents a task. People with ADHD tend to make piles of collected things and mix them all up with magazines, catalogs and bills; everything gets lumped in. If they recognize that a given piece of paper represents a "to do," they can quickly translate: it is a task. And then they can put it in their system and throw out the paper, or they can file the paper physically - or otherwise do what they want with it. Sometimes, it is helpful to have the paper to refer back to.

But generally, people want to have all the information in their systems, even that which they do not even need. They are like to look at the paper, figure out what the task is, and then put it in their digital box. It is the same with email. I have seen many adults use email as a task management system. If somebody sent me an email, I would go back to my email inbox to figure out what I have to do with it. The problem is that emails are for communication and not a task management tool. Here again, they have to separate the tasks. They get an email and they create a task for it before moving it to their trusted system.

Then the email can be answered, "okay, I will take care of this. I will let you know when I am done." They can delete it or save it as a reference. But now that task is no longer buried in their email. They have it in a system they can easily manage.

So the goal is to have more than one but not more than two to-do lists or collection systems. No need to move everything into one digital inbox or everything gets printed on paper to be stored in one cardboard box. People with ADHD have difficulty with executive functions. This means, among other things, that they have difficulty holding multiple pieces of information in their minds at the same time. People with ADHD need to prioritize all the hundreds of things they have to take care of at some point. Which one is the most important? Which one are they going to take action on next? But, unfortunately, they cannot do that. If they have multiple systems, there is just no way to hold all this in their minds and make intelligent choices.

If they have one system, they can lay it out visually. I like the phone apps specially made for people with ADHD. For example, drag and drop apps. Other systems are recommended for people with ADHD to deal with the idea of an "inbox"

Any software systems recommended as a main collection system has to be easy to use and makes sense to the user. I know people who using phone apps, and I also know people who love notebooks. They will acquire a notebook with high-quality paper and a fancy pen. They might have pictures in it that work great since they like to open such a book.

Other people are good with a phone app or use spreadsheets. I had one guy who put stuff on baseball cards to managed his tasks. I thought that was brilliant. So for people with ADHD, any system that works is best for them.

Some have a cloud-based system, and there is a special version for people with ADHD. Then there is a phone version. They can also run it on ta tablet. It is super handy because most of us carry our phones around with us all the time. They can quickly put stuff when they get the idea of having to do something. It has a computer interface so if they are often at a computer, they have this big screen and can drag things around with their mouse. It is very visual and very easy to use.

I am also a big fan of Google. People with ADHD can use Google tasks, an extension in Gmail. So they can have it right next to their Gmail. Emails are not tasks, but they can easily drag emails into Google tasks, and then it becomes a task.

I use another Google app called Google to keep not for tasks, but for keeping data, and anything important like a restaurant I want to remember. But for tasks, I prefer Google task.

If you are using Gmail, it is perfect and very easy. It is integrated with Google calendar. If you have a task with a due date, it will show up on your Google calendar. The interface is genuinely nice and clean.

Another system is the concept of "contexts." It means doing tasks specifically in a group. Apps like Tick Tick support tags while Microsoft outlook also does tags nicely. Google can tag a task like "make a call."

So now everything is in your system of choice. So, how do the person with ADHD approach it? How do they tackle their inbox? It starts with prioritizing and asking is this a long-term or a short-term thing.

Prioritizing tasks is like eating at a buffet restaurant. Their trusted system is a lot like a Chinese buffet. It is big and overwhelming. There are dishes of food all over the place, but they have only one plate. The metaphor is that the trusted system is the restaurant. So what they are doing today is their plate, and they look around and say, "okay, what am I going to eat right now? Or what am I going to do today?"

And they give themself a helping hand and put it on their plate; then they only look at their plate. They do not have to look at the rest of the stuff. Overwhelm is a big problem for people with ADHD, and it must be managed They can use high, medium, and low priority tags for their tasks, - a category or a tag called "today". If you intend to do it today, you will put that particular tag on the item. In the morning, ask what am I realistically going to accomplish today? What is important for me to do today? You then review the tasks with the "today tag" on them.

Deferring, delegating, trashing.

Trashing means deleting things, deciding what is not going to happen. But before deciding, you notify the relevant person. **Deferring** means "I am not going to do it right now. I am going to do it at some point in the future." You put the task on a "maybe someday list" for ideas you they do not want to lose and are not quite ready to let go. They are not ready to be dropped, so you are acknowledging their existence. Of course, you don't have to worry about them daily.

Delegating: most people with ADHD could use some improvement, even if it simply means asking for help to take care of something they are working on. The lucky ones among us have a system of help to rely on. But not all of us are blessed. People with ADHD have to be a bit more creative. Do they have the means to hire somebody to help them, say with their cleaning? Are their children ready to take on more responsibility? Who else can they get to help them? Ideally, they should be delegating things and focusing more on what they are good at. But that is another topic. Once they have their list of things that to do, they can sort them by priority or assign them to contexts or people - or whatever they want to do.

Every single task, once it is in the right place, has an action associated with it. I think people with ADHD get stuck with the thought, "What am I going to do?" Deferring it to someone else is often is a good idea, but if not, just file it. Nonetheless, it important to get support, be able to handoff things, and drop or trash them.

It is not as straightforward as it may seem.. It means making decisions about how important the task is and if it something to do right now? Keep in mind that if people with ADHD find something overly complicated, they are not going to do it. Make it simple and do what works for them; use the basic principles. As noted, what works best is to have two inboxes, a physical one for papers and the digital one (Google tasks). You have to combat the ever-present ADD forgetfulness like moving the stuff, so the physical task into a digital system is hard.

Some people with ADHD can use meditation, relaxation techniques, and nutrition support for their symptoms. When people eat healthy foods, they let go of sugar or sometimes flour, gluten, artificial colors, and artificial sweeteners. These things, in some people, can trigger an ADD/ ADHD reaction. I had success with some clients who went off gluten, but it does not work for everybody.

ADHD is a spectrum of symptoms; people on the low end absolutely can be helped. Some of my clients do not even take ADHD meds: they use meditation and exercise. They are very serious about their nutritional habits too, and it work for them. These habits make them more mindful and more aware of what is happening in their brains How fast is your mind racing? Remember that it helps to slow down. Slowing down, focusing, and being mindful is good for all humans, not just for people with ADHD.

Chapter 12:
Eliminating Clutter

Declutter your mind

Sue West is a marvelous organizer and a certified organizational coach. She has recently written a new book called, Organized for Fresh. I am very much impressed by the book; and in this chapter, we will discuss organization and decluttering for people with ADD/ADHD.

Not everybody that exhibits cluttering and hoarding has ADHD, but a large percentage do. It is such a struggle for these people. There is never a one-size-fits-all solution. The solution is different for different people. They have various processing modalities. Let us start with the first one, which is visual.

Modalities

Some people cannot figure out how to do something unless they have drawn a picture of it. You might be describing a house you went to and where the rooms were, what was in the rooms, or how the desk was placed in relation to the chair. They have to draw it because that is how they see it.

They cannot grasp things with a good sense of time until they put see them visually. I was with a client recently; we are trying to go through an entire house. We took a whiteboard, and put the weeks on it. We wrote down the steps in the bigger picture because many people with ADHD have a stronger visual sense than the average person. In fact, that is pretty common. Most people think they are more visually inclined than other people while others might be more auditory.

It is an easier way for people to organize what is going on in their heads by using computer programs. You have heard the term "hyper-focus". The issue is to look for one email then you leave if for two hours because you are on Facebook. People with ADHD should set a timer when they go on Facebook or any other social network site whether it is 10 or 15 minutes to make sure they don't spend too much time.

Along with visual and auditory modalities, you have taste and smell, and the emotional and cognitive intuitive. When I think of sensory modalities, emotions are the strongest and most fascinating ones. People with ADHD are highly emotional. I was working with a client a few years ago who was into sewing and quilting. So she had a lot of fabric. You have to find a way to connect such individuals emotionally to discern they are trying to declutter and sort out. You must help them make up their minds first to let go at some point. They might have said, "I do not want to have as much and I want to simplify," and then at the same time, their thoughts are, "I cannot find my favorites. I want to keep them all."

Some of the emotional techniques I ended up using included moving the emotional attachment to things to a whole new level. so the client picked up one of the fabrics and said, "I would never marry this fabric. It is just not handsome enough". I replied, "Yes, you are right." And she kept going. She picked up another piece of fabric and said, "Now this one, I know never in a million years would I marry it. I should throw it out of here." Then there were fabrics in between that she would not get rid of. They could "stay here for a while."

She had this whole story because she was so connected to her fabrics, using the concept of getting married or getting a divorce. This how she tried to organize her stuff. "I am going to marry you," "I will let you live here "and "you are out of here," It was perfect for her because she had a very heavy emotional attachment.

Another case was a lady client who inherited a lot of furniture from relatives, and she had intense relationships with every one of the pieces. She wanted to get rid of them, but she could not because she loved the people to whom they originally belonged. So I advised her to do grief work and then either sell them or give them away. But she was so into the relationship and the emotional connection was so strong that she was stuck. Although she started making some progress, I could see that she was still in the processing category, a very emotional phase where many people will say, "well, if I get rid of this object, this piece of furniture, this shawl, whatever it is, I feel like I am throwing myself away."

And that is it. Emotional people will say, "I feel like I am dishonoring the memory of the person who gave that to me. So my mother knitted me this beautiful blanket. And if I throw the blanket off, it is like I am throwing a part of my mother away, and I might not remember her anymore."

It is the main cognitive distortion. I always ask people, what was the essence of your mother? Then can we make a memory box and keep five or six of her items instead of everything. They do have to go through the grief process to be ready to let go of some things and get back into their own lives. I get people ready to the point where they can let go of someone dear to them.

I am not a personal organizer. I am not helping them with their shelves or with arranging their stuff. But I do know how to work through the grief. Once they get the grief go and out all the baggage, they can work with an organization system successfully versus spending six months trying to get ready in a mechanical way.

It can be frustrating for the organizer and for themselves. I often get people on the tail end of a life change when something major has happened. The husband has a heart attack, somebody had knee surgery, a parent died. The kids are gone and they enter the empty nest phase. I get them at "the end of the phase "when they are not quite processing and ready for the next chapter. They do not know what it looks like. Big transitions in life are so stressful; and the more memories you have, the more stressful it becomes.

It can be overwhelming. All life changes never come in singles: they always come several in a row. The universe has its own way of putting a greater impact on you. It becomes a thousand times more difficult for persons with ADD/ADHD.

When someone tells me that he/she had got ADHD, my first question is always, "Do you have a diagnosis, or why do you think you have ADHD? Anxiety can look like ADHD. Lots of things can look like ADHD. So if the person has organizing issues, we talk about how the ADHD showed up for them. It is very different for different people.

One of the other questions I ask is, "Are you taking medications, and are you taking them regularly?" One of the issues with ADHD has to do with working memory, especially short-term memory. It does not function very well as part of one's neurology.

If patients with ADHD are taking meds to help them with the distraction and memory issue, they are always concerned because with every medication, there is a side effect. Even today, we do not even have the medical technology to study the long-term effects of these meds.

On some people, they do not work. So I always ask, "are you willing to try new habits? That is what a lot of this is about. "Are you willing to practice some of the ideas that I give you or come up with together? Do you admit you have ADHD? Do you accept it? And are you at least willing to work with me so we can embrace it and make it part of you?"

One of the things you hear about people with ADHD is that they need diversity. They love new stuff. They do not like the maintenance phase. I try to embrace it, saying, "let's not have the same structure to your days, five days a week." Many entrepreneurs and business owners have ADHD. It is perfect because every single day is so different. It is a perfect fit with things changing every day. It is a different schedule every day - never the same. So people with ADHD fit in well in a business setting. The bad fit would be someone who has to sit at a computer all day and do data entry. Any desk job for an ADD/ ADHD person is a tough unless they are writing, being creative with graphic design or doing something different.

Let's talk about how to address people about their strengths and get them on the strength wagon versus the train of pain - which goes on and on and on. It makes them worse and worse, but they have been living with it their whole lives. I know a lady who was diagnosed in her late thirties with ADHD. I remember when she said it was such a relief to understood why she did not do well in school, left, and got into debt. It explained her horrendous health issues? It is a relief at first.

You may have a lifelong bout of low self-confidence and low self-esteem. The big thing is figure out what is working well for you in the past to get organized. How do you keep things together at work, and what can you learn and use at home? So, I help people find the good pieces to what they are doing - the good strategies, the good ways. Good here means effective ways, the ones we want to we bring them into our homes and offices.

No one is a disorganized person instinctively. It is all about ADHD neurology. But there are also some benefits of having ADHD. These p people are good multitaskers. In addition, ADHD brings positive things in terms of flexibility and kindness.

In comparison, an accountant who has to sit the whole day can be just fine. They can do the rote work very effortlessly and smoothly, and even be creative. In my coaching program, I had a man and a woman at different stages of life. One of them called it a disorder while the other one called it a gift. I loved that. I think it is better to have a gift because then you are not a victim. A disorder sounds like something is wrong with me.

Okay, I understand. There is a problem in the brain, and they just hit a brick wall. It has been happening in their brain for years. People with ADHD, especially children, were often coded as having oppositional defiance disorder. Once you use a certain label, it becomes really hard. It becomes an identification for a person's whole makeup, which is terrible. I have worked with many people with ADHD, but they have not told their employer because other people might think it is a reason for getting special treatment.

I explain it to people in simple terms Think about a classical orchestra with all these instruments. The conductor glues everybody together, making sure one section is quieter when require. If he is the leader, imagine taking him away. You would have chaos, and that is what happens in the ADHD brain. There is no conductor. The ADHD brain is not where you should to prioritize. Plan all the steps out to whatever your project is and then you can order them.

Declutter your environment

Decluttering is a process with an end goal. We want to get rid of stuff. We want to make our environment cleaner. We want to make sure that we are not overwhelmed. So when we look at that pile of laundry piling up in the corner, we do not feel like doing it because it is a big job.

I am going to give you tips to help. First, suppose you are not the type of person who loves to clean. Start with cleaning for five minutes or ten minutes per day; whichever it is, start small.

Although it is not something you are enthusiastic about, you have to break it down into segments. "I am going to go and clean for ten minutes." Use this plan to clean your house or a room. Record the time. Then you can say "I am done with my 10 minutes for the day." Or you might take a break and come back and do another 10 minutes - Whatever you need to do to get you in the mood to start cleaning.

Say to yourself, "I know it is a priority, and I will want to do something else in the next 30 minutes." Do not say, "I am just not going to do it because that looks like a big task."

It is better to say, "Hey, I will clean for five or 10 minutes and then see where I am." You can do that, and you might go past the time and not notice, thinking "I am in the process of cleaning. I know that I can go into the next five minutes." But if you are not that enthusiastic person, you are likely to say, "okay, I am just going to start with five minutes or 10. I will work on this one section of the room or work on this one section of the closet, whatever it is right."

Then you start doing it for five minutes or 10 minutes. Maybe you take a break and come back and do another five or 10 minutes. "I am going to do this much. I am going to do three sets of 10." It sounds like lifting weights since you are doing three sets of 10 minutes. So do three sets of 10 minutes: go in and clean for 10 minutes, take a break, come back clean for another 10 minutes, take a break, come back clean for another 10 minutes, take a break, etc.

Try to do one task or item per day. Say you have ten different pots and pans, but you never use like five of them. Give at least one away, whether you donate it or give it as a gift to a friend. Throw it away if you have to, but get rid of one item per day. If you get rid of one item per day, you will get rid of 365 items in a year. I am not saying stuff you need; I am referring to that chair with a broken leg. You intended to fix it, but you never did. And matter of fact, you have not fixed it for so long that you have bought another to replace it. But that one chair is still sitting in the living room. Throw that chair out, get rid of it, give it to somebody else who wants to fix it, or donate it.

That is your one item for that day, so try to find other items you do not need and are not important to you. You may be the person who is a blessing to somebody else. You may say, "I have never worn this. It is still in pretty good condition. I will see if so-and-so needs it." And then they can use it. Otherwise, it just kind of sits there and takes up space. You are trying to figure out how to make more space to have a cleaner, and neater-looking living area.

The 12 by 12 by 12 challenge

The next thing is going to sound a little strange, but I promise you it is worth it. It is the 12 by 12 by 12 challenge. First, you pick 12 things to throw out. Second, you pick 12 things to donate. And third, you pick up 12 items off the floor or around the house and find a proper place for them. How is this going to help? It is going to eliminate 36 items around your house or apartment that make for clutter. It is going to help clean your house. If you are committed and you find this fun, go ahead and do another 36 the next day until you get down to a place where you do not have a lot of clutter.

You are just giving away or throwing away stuff, but it will reduce the number of items in your house. You are finding proper places for the other items, making your house or apartment cleaner and more organized. Maybe you cannot get to the 12 the first time. Maybe you think, "I do not want to give away 12. I will do ten but try to get to that 12 because that will help you."

If you want to do it more than one day, go ahead and do it again. The second day of the third day -however many days you want to keep getting rid of things to keep organized - then go ahead and do that. But at least do the first part, which is the 12 by 12 by 12 challenge. I think it is great because it will help you get rid of 24 items and put 12 items back in their place.

If you look at an item and ask if it brings you joy, and the answer is no, you should to think about getting rid of it. "Do I love this item? Do I use this item? Do I think I need this item? Think about the last six months to a year. You do not want to hold on to items for forever.

"I needed it at one time. I do not need it now, but I might need it again." It could be a generator and you say, "Hey, I need that." But what about some of the other stuff that you do not love, have never worn, or have never used. You say, "I have never even thought about these things for ages." The initial response to the challenge are many.

If you get stuck, ask a friend for help. It should not be "can you help me move stuff?" Because if you ask a friend for something onerous, they may not show up. No one likes the process of moving. You do not like it in general. They may help you because they like you even if they are loathe to do it. Of course, if it is reasonable, they will rush to help you.

Having another person in the room motivates you to do whatever you need to do. It is a sound theory to have a body double (not like an evasion of the body snatchers kind of thing). It is not like you have a doppelganger. So have other people in the room to motivate the team. You are aware that they are there and what you are supposed to be doing. Don't feel guilty. "I need to do this thing. I invited them over, and I have not done what I invited them over to help me with." So if they are good friends, they will help you through the process and decide about tasks and priorities. They no doubt have ideas about clutter and organization.

But just having a friend come over and hang out, sitting in the room, is not true help. You have to get on the next point. It may be breaking things down into segments or another system. You don't want to procrastinate and get demotivated. Help with processing tasks can be simple and effective. Something that once took two hours can take only ten minutes. Then you'll be more inspired to accomplish it because you won't be feeling overwhelmed and think, "oh, I have all this stuff due.

The amount of time is limited to complete a task. Don't say "It will take me three hours" and opt for, "Hey, I have to do 10 minutes. And if I feel like doing another 10 minutes, I will do that." Create a checklist to keep you on track. If you have ADHD, you need reminders. That is what a checklist is for. You can have a checklist for how much time you need to spend cleaning. You can have a checklist for most anything to make sure it is done and done on time.

So you want to create a checklist. When you have completed things, y9ou tick them off the list. You are going to feel good because now you have completed something and can enter your reward system. It helps to release dopamine, which always imparts a good feeling.

You can always set a timer. This goes back to the 10-minute thing. How will you know if you have done the 10 minutes unless you have a timer. Use a timer, a stopwatch, whatever works. You want to have a method to indicate that you have completed something. You will be able tell that a 10-minute session has been done or 20 minutes have elapsed. It could even be your break. You want to have a timer with you and a checklist to help you stay on track.

You can also benefit from labeling. If you do not label things, you will put something away and have no idea where it is, or you will put it in a special place that you forget about. Make sure you are labeling whatever you are putting away. when you start to declutter, say, "okay, I will keep this and put it in this box. I am putting it in this container." When you want to get those things out, if you don't label the location, you will have no idea where they are. You have to go the digging process. If you ever have put up Christmas lights, you know about this. Did you put the same types of things in one container? It is important because you only take them out once a year. What happens is we try to find things the next year. "I do not know where the lights are." You are trying to remember what box they are in. Labeling can save oodles of time and anxiety. So, again, label things.

The next thing I would recommend is to stash clear storage bins. Anything labeled means it is easy to find when the time comes. You can look at them and say, "oh, the Christmas lights are in here". You can see into clear storage bins. This is more about just being organized; it will help you declutter. Things are out of sight but you know where they are. The bins and the labels both work together to help you clean up your space and stay organized.

I like to say, "out of sight, out of mind." If you are trying to remember where you put something and you need that thing, hopefully it was stored in a labeled bin where you can see it. Otherwise, You will never know it is there. You may have forgotten that you even bought it.

You want a way to see what you have put in a bin or box. Any visual cue will help you if you have ADHD. If you do not want to lose or misplace things, make sure you can see them when you are looking. In short, make sure they are visual so your eyes will cross over them. You don't have to remember where they are if you can see them. So out of sight out of mind has to do with things you pack away to declutter. But your system brings them back to your line of sight.

When tacking anything, make sure that you have all the things that you need in front of you. Have it all in your visual field. Then when you look at them, you can say, "Hey, everything is here." That will help proceed more efficiently without wracking your brain.

The last thing I am going to say is that you should remove distractions when you are trying to declutter. Put down your phone, and do not answer it where you placed it. You may get distracted by an interesting post on Facebook or another social platform. Obsession with social media is rampant, ADD or not.

Get rid of all distractions. Get off your tablet and close that laptop. Do not watch your favorite TV program while you are trying to declutter. Maybe put on some music that is not particularly distracting so that you can focus on the process.

I hope these tips help you get into the declutter and process and make your environment cleaner and more organized. It will lower the overwhelm to going through a systematic organization process.

Chapter 13:
Curbing Impulsivity and Money Issues

I n psychology, impulsivity (or impulsiveness) is the inclination to act on an impulse, with little or no forethought, analysis, or consideration of the consequences. Impulsive behaviors are often "poorly planned, prematurely expressed, overly dangerous, or unsuited to the situation that frequently result in unpleasant results," risking long-term goals and success tactics. Thus, impulsivity can be thought of as a multifactorial construct.

However, a functional form of impulsivity has also been proposed, that entails impulsive actions in inappropriate conditions resulting in beneficial outcomes. "When such activities have positive effects, they are viewed as marks of boldness, agility, spontaneity, daring, or unconventionality, rather than impulsivity." Thus, the concept of impulsivity comprises at least two independent components: first, behaving without sufficient forethought, which may or may not be effective, and second, preferring short-term rewards over long-term ones.

In this chapter, we are going to talk about how to curb impulses and help your relationships if you have ADHD. We will discuss a little bit about why people with ADHD tend to spend more money than others. They tend not to save up as much as a result.

Curbing impulsive spending

How you can decrease the chances of impulsive spending? That question may apply to any impulsive behavior if you have with ADHD. Of equal importance is how to cope with these issues in a relationship given that the biggest things that couples fight over are sex, kids, and money. It takes open communication in a non-punitive way non-judgmental way. You can feel more confident about finances. Say you have parents with ADHD who did not have a good handle on money. It could be a challenge to figure out how to handle your finances when the people you lived with growing up had a frustrating relationship them. Both partners in a relationship have different family histories with money, which makes a difference in how you interact. Getting treatment for ADHD, particularly with stimulant medication, is the most effective kind of treatment, according to research. So how can that help you financially?

You may identify with some of the common ADHD financial issues. A higher rate of debt in the general population was found in a study by Russell Barkley. He discovered that people with ADHD have a higher rate of debt, particularly credit card debt, and a higher rate of bankruptcies and foreclosures along with increase relationship difficulties due to money. If you have ADHD, you are more likely to get divorced; you are more likely to remarry and get divorced again. Sometimes impulsive spending can play into relationship issues such as the disorganization of financial papers. Say you are in the hospital and your family needs access to your financial documents; they do not know where they are on your computer or where the hard copies are stored, and it can cause a lot of stress for family members.

The person with ADHD lacks investments and/or ways to save for the future. Most people wish to retire at a certain age and live off their earnings, but people with ADHD have difficulty seeing that far ahead. And people with ADHD tend to be underemployed, which means they are employed below their ability. If you have a job where you are not meeting job expectations, you leave that job or are fired and you start at the same level of employment. In essence, you tend to not rise through the ranks. It is much more difficult for people with ADHD to get promoted. Hence, experience underemployment, having struggles with making ends meet many times. It can be exceedingly difficult to save up for the future and, of course, with the pandemic, it is even more difficulty to lose jobs and thrive.

Also, consider all the late fees for non-payment of bills. We will talk about how to get your bills set up on an electronic sending machine so you do not have to think about them; you just have to make sure that you have enough money in your account when the funds are withdrawn. A lower credit score is typical for people to ADHD and thus they often get turned down for loans. It may be for school, an emergency, or other critical need. It hurts not to qualify and greatly increases the amount of stress.

A recent study shows that if you have ADHD, you have a shortened lifespan compared to other people because of the stress and related health conditions. They can get worse if you aren't getting your financial needs met. Foreclosures can occur with chronic unemployment or being underemployed at a lower pay than you deserve and require.

People with ADHD tend to be people pleaser to cover-up who they are and blend in. They have a hard time taking criticism and negotiating deals or a salary increase. They don't negotiation skills or even realize that they can ask for money without embarrassment.

A lot of self-esteem issues, guilt and shame get wrapped up with ADHD. But why do people have difficulties with paying their bills? Such executive functions as budgeting and attending to bills are mostly in the frontal lobe of the brain. They include taking in information and deciding what is important. These functions in the brain can be impaired with ADHD. You may have impairment in different areas of executive functioning. You may have a friend with ADHD and their ADHD looks a little different than yours. Different symptoms show up, so planning what you need to work on will have to adapt to circumstances. What works for you doesn't always work for others.

For example, initiating tasks and getting motivated is not a problem for normal persons. On the other hand, motivation and attention is a problem for many with ADHD. So, you may be ready to do something, but your brain does not have enough oomph to go ahead and do it. Thus, it is very difficult to get started on tasks, especially tasks you are not interested in. It is as if someone wakes up in the morning and says, "Oh, I want to create a budget, that sounds like fun fun." It is really dry and just not exciting, and your brain is like right – you either are under-attentive or hyper-focused.

So you have issues paying attention, or your attention is laser short to the point where somebody can be calling your name and you are not answering because you are so into what you are doing. It is an issue with regulation and motivation, not with attention.

Yu can learn from consequences of your actions, but you forget what the outcome was and repeat the behavior because it was satisfying and fun. With impulsive spending, you get a high credit card bill and have difficulty paying it down. So, the next time you're having a bad day, you go shopping and feel better because you get a boost of dopamine and serotonin, which are low in the ADHD brain. Thus, shopping is a form of self-medication. So you go ahead and shop again, your credit card bill goes up even more, is really difficult for the ADHD brain

to connect behavior to consequences if you have an impulsive nature. Again, you had a bad day and shopping temporarily made you feel better. You do not think about the remorse you had later on. There is also a high rate of math learning disabilities with ADD. If you look at the numbers related to your finances, sometimes those numbers can flip on you and you write them backward. You see a number that does not look like what it actually is. A lot of issues related to money processing are just reading about financial stuff. It may be difficult for you to sit and read so an audiobook may be more helpful.

I usually recommend to people to read for at least 10 minutes daily. The subject does not matter. Get into the mode of feeling comfortable; if you can get the material in audio format, that is even better. If you are an adult with ADHD, you have significantly more executive function impairment than people without it. If you have a high IQ, you can compensate somewhat, but you still have just as much executive function impairment as someone with an average IQ.

Now we are doing a lot of online shopping. If you have been good about keeping quarantine during the panic, there are some general rules. But it is still easy to splurge. When you are in a relationship, you have a joint checking account which can cause some issues because you may be spending money and not telling your partner. You may be doing what I call sneaky spending: you are spending but hiding it. I call it financial infidelity because you know that you are going to get in trouble if you tell your partner, "Hey, I just spent like a thousand dollars on this TV." Instead, you let it slide right but it can adds up and the guilt and shame ensue. You avoid and communication and the possible arguments waiting to erupt.

I tell people is to wait 24 hours and then make a purchase. But before that, learn a little more. Read up on how Amazon and other online retailers are set up to make you spend money. It is pretty fascinating how they have used what is called consumer psychology to get you to spend money. Once you learn their tricks are, it is easier to step back because you know the manipulation component is to get you to spend and spend. Go shopping with a friend that maybe does not have ADHD or is not impulsive and says, "Hey, you know, do you really need that thing? Do you really think that might be a good idea?"

It is a nice gentle way to remind you to kind of stop and think. Go shopping on off-hours. If you're in a crowd, like the day after Thanksgiving and everybody is going crazy, you jump in following the herd mentality. Our brains tells us that we need to do what everybody else is doing. So remember – off-hours.

Is excessive impulsivity biologically programmed? So go shopping where there are as few people as possible. There is less sensory stimulation too. Grocery stores are rough for people with ADHD because instead of three kinds of cereal, you have 500. You can stay on the cereal aisle or start talking to yourself out loud. If you are noticed, it becomes more than a little embarrassing. You are standing in front of all these cereals, and you do not know which one to pick. You would rather choose from three rather than 500. Before you go to the grocery store, you can order online.

A lot of grocery stores provide online services. They will put the groceries right in your cart; that is a safer right now during the pandemic in any case. Also when you go to the grocery store, set a time and go during off-hours. There is less stress when there is a lot less sensory input. Stop and look at your cart before you check out and ask yourself, "Do I really need this thing? Is this a need or a want? Was this on my grocery list, or is this just something I saw?"

Do you know the reason why you have candy and other bad things at the checkout? It is about impulse buying. Read up about consumer psychology. It is fascinating how retailers used the brain works to get you to spend money, so you want to look at your cart before checking out. "Do I need this stuff? Is this a frivolous purchase? Is this something I cannot live without?" Like milk: you may need milk but buy a kitchen tool that you will use like once a year, and you certainly do not need that. It is just something fun. So take those things out of your cart and just put them somewhere or give them to the cashier and say, "hey, I do not need this."

These people will be more than happy to take it away from you if you didn't want it. When you go back to put them away, you take up more time. You are also more likely to buy more stuff. So stick only to items on your list. Just uncheck it. Do meal planning on Sunday and think about what you will eat for the rest of the week and then buy accordingly. You will wind up spending a lot less money, especially when you have ADHD. After all, you tend to cook something quick because you do not want to mess with attention issues. You can plan your meals for the full week on Sunday and start eating healthily. Turn off your one-click ordering on Amazon which is designed to make you spend money. Beware of big sales; sometimes retailers bump up the item's price and then make it look like they have taken a percentage off.

Having human contact, even if you do not want to talk with people, does something to the brain psychologically. It is necessary for survival like having a place to live, clothing, water, food. These are the things that you need to include in your budget and can't be left out. But it is not the same for a really expensive steak something else. We can adapt our survival needs, but it can be hard to curb any splurges. If you have cable then why add Netflix? Still, it is pretty good to have Netflix because you can talk to others about something in common. But you can also invest your time in other healthy activities like exercising or outdoor sports. It is a matter of making wise choices.

Similarly, going to the spa, out for entertainment or to eat is a want that is not a need; you can get food somewhere else like your grocery store and you don't have to pay extra for that service. So take a look at what you are buying and distinguish a want from a need. I am not saying to eliminate the wants because we do need to treat ourselves sometimes, but we need to do it with moderation. I know moderation is tricky with ADHD. We are like, "Oh, a little bit of this thing is fun," but then a lot more of it is going to be even more fun. You do not think about it again until it comes around. The consequence is that you wind up paying a higher credit card payment or have issues with your partner.

Not using credit cards responsibly or not paying off your credit cards every month is like having a high-interest loan. If you have a lower credit score, you may have a credit card with a high interest rate. You can negotiate your interest rate by calling the credit card issuer. Some of the credit card companies have been pretty good about this and are pretty easy to work. Because of the pandemic, a lot of people have lost their jobs, so you can call the card issuer and tell them you are in debt. They will likely work out a payment plan with you. However, you want to be sure that it won't affect your credit.

Also, online purchases, do not use a debit card. You cannot guarantee that someone is not going to hack in and take money out of your bank account. If you use a credit card, you have some protection against fraudulent purchases. If you use a debit card, that money is gone, and it is harder to get it back. You can get a separate credit card not connected to your bank account just for online purchases. Also, lower your credit limit; if you feel like you will go over your credit limit, drop the purchase.

You need to look at credit cards as like using cash. We think that money is coming out of our accounts, but it is not coming out right away. We must use them responsibly. There are some cases where you need to use a credit card to build up your credit, but you may often find that you do not need one. Budgeting to people with ADHD is a really bad word.

Budgeting is not supposed to be fun; it is just a guideline for spending and saving. You need to know how much money you have on hand. Financial health comes from spending less. You have some money saved to the side for emergencies. You want about six months of living expenses and savings, so even if you put in five-ten dollars from every paycheck in the savings, that counts. You want to try to live under your means and not according to how much you make. It is how much you get to take home. You want to hold onto as much money as you can. You have reasonable spending habits and retain some money for the future.

You do not need math skills to create a budget. There are a lot of online budgets. If you have a math learning disability, numbers can be daunting, but you do not have to do any math now that we have good budget apps. It does it for you, so it is a dynamic budget, not static, which means that things can change from month to month.

You may need to spend more on dental visits one month if you need ex-rays and you do not have dental insurance. It is not necessary to visit the dentist the next month, but you should ensure that you have enough money in your "pot" so when you do visit the dentist, you do not go overboard. So, you have these big costs and all of a sudden, you think, "Oh no, where am I going to get this big money from to pay this thing.

Take your expenses and divide them by 12. Put a little bit in each pot every month. You will have a lot less stress because when you do need that money, It is there when you need it for things like car repairs. Once you start building up your assets and decreasing your debts, you will see your money last longer. There is a way to determine your net worth, basically how much money you have after expenses? It can be really scary to figure out what you have if you are out of control and fail to budget.

Conflicts over money tend to be one of the biggest things couples fight about in marriage ADD or not. Money is usually one of the issues they need to discuss, and they tend to have more emotions with them. Now money does not have a prefixed emotional value; it is the value we attach to it, and some of that has to do with what our relationship with money.

To find out your relationship to money and how you value it, ask questions. Are you a spender? Are you a saver? Can the two of you in the marriage work together and work through those past relationships with money and come to a healthy understanding that works for you as a couple. When people with ADHD are in the midst of a divorce due to financial issues like impulsive spending, they each have different money histories. Open communication is key, and you need a partner who is willing to discuss the matter in a non-punitive, non-punishing way. You can talk about money without it devolving into a fight. If you are arguing about money, it may really concern who has more power in the relationship or more spending ability. It is not always what you think.

I recommend that couples meet at least an hour every week to discuss what I call housekeeping, including money, to provide the data for their joint schedule. It is important to revisit the schedule. Again, be aware of sneaky spending, that overspending you try to hide it from your spouse because if they find out, it will not end well. And again, sometimes people find that they are with someone who cannot have rational discussions. It is not the only sign that there is an issue with the marriage: usually it is a sign of other problems too.

Communication is difficult. Some couples keep separate accounts to avoid conflict. You can do your accounts any way you want while joint accounts create a lot of problems for people with ADHD. If you are not tracking your money or using a budgeting app, you may forget to record your expenditures. You will continually irritate your partner, especially one who is frugal and organized.

I always recommend using an online money tracking app. If you keep separate accounts, the two of you can spend your own money without having to check in with each other. If you forget, it is okay but make sure your partner has access to your personal account in case of an emergency. You can ask your bank how to set it up. Most couples have to deal with emergences like some type of incapacitation. If you die, your partner or another designated person has access to your money. It can be part of a living will or results from having power of attorney. You can talk to an attorney or search online for information.

By keeping separate accounts, I see many couples do much better and they are on time with paying the mortgage or rent. Sometimes, the couple splits expenses at a ratio of 50/50. Sometimes they split it by some percentage of their combined income. Somebody might be bringing in 60 of the revenue, so the other person makes 40. They pay proportionately, or they can use another system.

"Hey, I will cover the rent if you can cover utilities and streaming services" or ... whatever. Couples handle budgeting in different ways, but it always helps to have someone with you when you are talking about it, at least in the beginning. There are a couple of rules here: stick to the subject, you cannot bring up any past issues, and no name-calling. If you need to step away because your anger is raising your frustration, you can say, "Hey, I need about 10 minutes," and go for a walk. When you have ADHD, it also helps if your medicine is on board. It is you and your partner against the big money issue. It is not you against your partner; keep that in mind.

Here is another common scenario: you are spending money on religious activities without a proper check and balance. If you have hugely different views about how much money you are going to give to your religious entity or how often, there could be a disagreement between the two of you. It may be something you can sit down and talk about at the kitchen table or with your counselor or religious leader. But again, you know that in the end, money is not good or bad. It just is the value we ascribe to money that is at stake. So if the household money is being used for something you both are not morally okay with, that is a top priority to resolve as a couple's issue.

Whoever is more organized or has a background in finances might want to be put in charge of the money, but the other person still has equal financial rights. Sometimes, there is financial abuse in relationships, where one person says, "Well, you have ADHD and cannot handle the money." So they take over tracking the money and the other person cannot access it or even ask what is in the accounts. They are given an allowance. That constitutes financial abuse. You as the ADHD person have the right to know what is always going on with your money. If money is used as an incentive in the relationship and held as a reward or punishment, it is time to go to couple's therapy.

There is a type of therapy where you have the therapist in the room and also a financial professional or advisor. Hence, the therapist has the therapy part, and the financial person handles the money part. In one study, couples with ADHD found this to be very helpful. They could talk about their money issues with people who represented each part of the issue. It is a very sound type of approach to therapy.

ADHD requires stimulant medication. With 30-40 years of study are logged, stimulant medication is still the most effective treatment for ADHD versus non-stimulant medication alone. It gives you time between an impulse buy and thinking about it. Sometimes just those split seconds assist you in making a better decision, one in your best interest. It also helps you with as a filter during money discussions, especially if your frustration level goes up. It also helps delay that instant gratification at the heart of overspending or any type of excess. If you are not treating your ADHD, you are more likely to go with CBT or cognitive behavioral therapy, especially if you have guilt and shame about money. You can talk with someone about it. A therapist can assist you in resolving these issues, and CBT is quite effective in treating ADHD.

So is there hope for getting healthy with financial issues? A lot of people are in a crisis nowadays due to the pandemic, but please get your ADHD evaluated and seek good treatment. If you feel that your treatment is not working, talk to your prescriber or therapist and see if you can get on a better track with your medicine.

If you can afford to get an assistant, have somebody help you with day-to-day tasks. Maybe it is just helping with filing, scanning or whatever you need to stay on track. Seek help from both mental health and financial professionals. There are financial professionals who specialize in working with ADHD and their impulsivity issues. But be incredibly careful because some corrupt companies or individuals will say that they can handle your debt, but they also charge you for it; so really educate yourself about that.

Instead of getting your bills at home through the mail paper, make sure everything is electronic. A lot of people are doing electronic billpaying. Take a chunk out of your day, like an hour or two, to go through and turn all your statements into electronic documents. It save a lot of paper piling up. It is fast and easy to elect automatic deposit and withdrawal.

You can get a certain percentage automatically deposited from your paycheck into a savings account. It is a quick way to save money without even missing it. More and more articles about money and couples with an ADHD partner are coming out every year. This has become a really big topic, especially right now during the pandemic when people's financial situations have changed so much. If you buy something, you feel pretty good until it does not feel good anymore, right? If you treat your ADHD, you are less likely to have those impulse purchases, which leads to less guilt and shame. In no time, it becomes a cycle of positivity.

Create a support system with the help of the right professionals. I have seen some people with ADHD do very well in managing their money. So, I think it depends on whether you are willing to ask for help or not. It also depends on how much time you take to educate yourself about the ways and means of money. remember that saving up the money puts into perspective how hard you work to earn a thing. That is a valuable lesson for anybody of any age.

Chapter 14:
Managing Emotions

I ndividuals are constantly exposed to potentially stimulating situations that have the potential to elicit an emotional reaction. These situations can be external (for example, receiving criticism or a compliment, seeing a newborn baby, or witnessing another person suffer) or internal (for example, thinking negatively or positively about yourself or thinking positively or negatively about your future).

The amount of attention a person devotes to potentially arousing a problem as well as their cognitive (mental) assessment of the circumstances - including the meaning and significance they give to the problem, and their level of confidence in their ability to deal with the situation - determine whether the situation elicits an emotional response in them. The power, intensity, and duration of an individual's emotional response, on the other hand, are determined by their emotional sensitivity and ability to self-regulate.

The following factors influence an individual's emotional sensitivity and ability to self-regulate:

- whether they have gotten enough sleep, eaten well, exercised, and participated in stress-relieving/relaxing activities, and so on.

- their executive function capacity, which determines emotional impulsivity (the possibility that a primary emotional reaction will occur in response to a stimulus and also the speed with which the emotional response will occur) and emotional control/inhibition competence.

- their habits or automatic reflexes

The fight or flight reaction

An emotional response is defined as an individual's behavior and bodily expression of personal sentiments in response to a circumstance that they view to be relevant. The internal physiological changes that occur in an individual's body because of the fight or flight response being triggered influence the behavior displayed by the individual when triggered emotionally (facial expression, body movement, eye contact, and verbal expression, like tone of voice, volume, and language, etc.). The fight or flight instinct is a natural protective mechanism. The physiological responses are many:

- heart rate and blood pressure rise.

- The peripheral blood vessels contract to direct blood flow to the heart, lungs, and brain.

- The pupils dilate to take in more light.

- he heart, lungs, and brain need more energy. Thus, blood glucose levels rise.

- adrenaline and glucose excite the muscles, causing them to tighten.

- the smooth muscle relaxes, allowing more oxygen into the lungs.

- There is a turn down effect of all non-essential functions (such as digestion and immunity).

When the fight or flight reaction is triggered, the individual will also have difficulty focusing on even little activities and will lose the ability to engage in their executive functions (which further limits their power to regulate their thoughts, words, actions, and emotions). Again, this is due to the brain entering the assault or escape mode.

Both real and imagined threats might elicit the fight or flight reaction. However, when an individual's flight or fight response is activated too easily or frequently in response to a perceived but imagined danger, problems might arise.

Emotional control

A person's emotional response might be either healthy or unhealthy in the sense that it can have a favorable or negative impact on goal achievement, social connections, health, and wellbeing. Emotions such as happiness, love, joy, and empathy, for example, can build, maintain, and strengthen interpersonal relationships with others. Conversely, experiencing and expressing socially unacceptable emotions such as wrath and aggression can disrupt or destroy interpersonal relationships and lead to social isolation.

Individuals rely on their emotional self-regulation skills to amplify or inhibit an emotional reaction and hence protect goal attainment (social relationships, health, and wellbeing).

Emotional regulation is defined as the automatic (unconscious) or conscious (conscious) processes involved in the start, maintenance, and alteration of an individual's emotional experience and expression.

According to Kola's (2009) Hypothetical Model of Emotional Sensitivity versus Emotion Regulation, the process of regulating one's emotions has two separate stages.

Thriving Despite ADHD

Emotional sensitivity versus emotion management is a hypothetical model. The initial stage of the reaction is referred to as the main reaction by Koole (2009). A human has (and frequently displays) an immediate raw emotional response to an event during this stage. An individual's emotional trigger sensitivity determines the strength and speed with which an initial reaction develops.

Following this basic reaction, Koole (2009) claims that individuals can modify and change their emotional responses to achieve goals and maintain interpersonal connections. Thus, secondary reaction refers to the emotional response that occurs because of the primary response.

Modulating and modifying one's predominant emotional response entails the following steps:

- tying a reward (that serves as motivation) to the effort of reducing/changing one's primary emotional reaction

- participating in self-regulatory efforts to intentionally reduce/moderate the predominant emotion (for example, speaking to oneself to self-soothe, shifting attention away from a provoking incident)

Working memory, problem-solving (including anticipation to foresee future outcomes of possible reactions), and planning abilities are used to organize the final secondary emotional response to be adaptive and supportive.

ADHD and emotional dysregulation

The prevalence of emotional dysregulation in ADHD children is believed to be between 24 and 50 percent. The prevalence of emotional dysregulation in individuals diagnosed with ADHD is considered to be over 70%. (Shaw et al., 2014)

Individuals with ADHD frequently struggle with mood regulation. These difficulties are regarded to have a considerably greater influence on an individual with ADHD's wellbeing and self-esteem than the fundamental symptoms of ADHD (hyperactivity-impulsivity and inattention).

Emotional dysregulation is defined as the inability to moderate one's emotional experience and expression, resulting in an overly emotional response. This overreaction is deemed inappropriate given the individual's developmental age and the social situation in which it occurs.

ADHD-related emotional dysregulation is hypothesized to be caused by poor executive function control, which contributes to an individual's (Barkley, 2015). Due to a lack of self-control, the afflicted might have a very explosive emotional trigger sensitivity and emotional impulsivity. So, there is a high degree of impatience, and low emotional impulsivity characterized by a low level of tolerance, anger/reactive violence, and temper tantrums.

They have difficulty self-regulating their predominant emotional response. Individuals with ADHD may have such intense, overpowering primary emotional reactions that it is difficult for them to suppress the emotion or temper and replace it with a secondary emotional response.

They have difficulty shifting their attention away from intense emotions. It can be difficult to lessen or modify a primary emotional response if you cannot focus away from intense feelings. Problem refocusing can also add to thinking rumination.

Due to weak working memory, they have difficulty self-soothing to moderate their predominant emotional response (i.e., self-expression and visual imagery are impaired.).

They display difficulties in organizing and carrying out an effective secondary response due to judging, openly manipulating, managing information, creating, and appraising various answers and their probable results, while also planning an appropriate response.

In short, people with ADHD are more prone to the following:

- emotions are felt and displayed more powerfully, particularly during interpersonal encounters which may be due to being overwhelmed by the emotion.

- getting extremely enthusiastic

- concentrating on the negative features of a task or event

- demonstrating irritation or fury by becoming verbally or physically hostile

- having social relationship issues such as social rejection, bullying, and isolation

- Experiencing marital and relationship troubles, relationship breakups, and divorce

- having difficulty meeting work or academic goals/requirements, get suspended or expelled from school, lose their job, or are not promoted

- become a victim of road rage and vehicle accidents

They have heightened psychological distress because of their emotional experience.

- They become anxious and/or depressed

- They have behavioral issues, get involved in crime, and be institutionalized

Why am I so easily irritated?

There are many triggers for irritation: getting cut off on the highway, your mother-in-law is criticizing your parenting, your boss is insisting on you working over the weekend, and your computer is failing in the middle of a 40-page report that has not been saved. What do all these things have in common? It is the power to elicit wrath - pure, unadulterated fury, the kind where you scream your head off and toss your phone against the wall. ADHD brains are not only more susceptible to this powerful experience, but they are also more turned off by it when it gets in their way.

What exactly is anger?

Sure, we all know what it is like to be angry, but do you know what's going on within your body when you're upset?? Anger is the body's natural reaction to a threat. So when we all had to be wary of lions, tigers, and bears in ancient times, our bodies acquired the acute ability to feel the danger and thus arose a powerful mechanism to fight the threat off, i.e., our fight/flight reaction.

This fight/flight reaction is activated deep inside the brain to prepare our bodies (and brains) to fight as hard as they can or leave as quickly as they can from a harmful scenario. We try everything we can to oppose (or flee) from harm as hard and as fast as we can. It causes us to breathe quickly and shallowly (so there is as much oxygen as possible in our muscles). It raises our heart rate (to get all that oxygen where it has to go) and even begins to block access to our frontal lobe (so we do not worry about our to-do list when we need to flee from a charging tiger). What comes from all of this preparedness? It can mount slowly and steadily or it can turn on instantly with the flip of a switch.

What is the source of your rage?

However, fury is only one manifestation of our bodies' "ready condition." So why do we get that sensation in our bodies and feel worried, terrified, or even excited at times, and then feel like we want to strangle the person in front of us with our bare hands at other times?

Blame.

Anger is classified as a secondary emotion by psychologists. That is, we feel it after we have felt something else. I know it does not always feel that way—sometimes it feels like there is nothing between you and your anger. But if you replayed that single second of your life in slow motion, you would notice a flash of another emotion right before the rage. Maybe it is fear? Frustration? Or perhaps dread?

We have that uneasy feeling, and we despise it. As a result, our brain searches for someone or anything to blame. When we locate the source of the problem, we may shift from the uncomfortable, agonizing, and ultimately helpless sensation of fear, irritation, or worry to the more energetic and action-oriented feeling of fury. What is the source of my sensitivity?

Recognizing Hypersensitivity and ADHD

It has been suggested that having a tag collection as a child is a guaranteed way to know if you have ADHD. Few things irritate an ADHD brain more than a nagging itch on the back of the neck, the tug of a too-tight waistband, the poke of an errant underwire, or the yelp of a nervous dog. All of the world's irritants function like sand in the mouth of an oyster, except that for ADHD brains, the irritation produces fury, frustration, distraction, and emotional overwhelm rather than a beautiful pearl.

Hypersensitivity is also known as hyper empathy syndrome, HSP, and sensory sensitivity, and it is common in ADHD patients. Hypersensitive people are easily overwhelmed by both physical and emotional stimulation. This can result in strong emotions such as fury, anger, and physical symptoms such as headaches and rashes.

Hypersensitive people are frequently made to feel insane. They are advised that they are "too sensitive" or need to "toughen up." However, the sensitivity that the ADHD brain perceives is not due to a character deficiency and cannot be toughened out. Instead, it is a symptom with a neurobiological basis. People with hypersensitivity have entire hypersensitive systems, making them far more prone to suffer from biological sensitivities such as asthma, eczema, and allergies.

Symptoms of ADHD hypersensitivity:

When hypersensitive is there ADHD brains are more prone to be swamped with and irritated by:

- a loud and sudden noise
- lights that are bright or flashing
- quick-moving objects
- strong smells
- excessive information
- coarse cloth or tags
- too-tight clothing
- hair rubbing against skin
- there are too many people (can cause claustrophobia)
- strong emotions (their own or others')
- minor squabbles or frustrations
- sensitivity to touch

What causes the ADHD brain to be extra sensitive? When you are contemplating something controversial, you know you should tell yourself, "absolutely, do not say that?" Then the words are out of your mouth before you have even finished that admonition? We frequently attribute this to a "lack of filtration." It is easy to notice a lack of filter in the interruptions, abrupt outbursts, and odd jokes from the ADHD brain.

However, the absence of a filter on the things going out implies the lack of a filter on the items coming in. As a result, everything becomes conscious—every noise, every sight, every sound, and every feeling. Neurotypical brains can adapt to such sensory information. For example, if they are wearing a watch, you may be aware of it for a brief moment, but you quickly stop detecting that it is there. There is no reason to do so. The brain shuts out consistent information to attend to more essential things, just as it does with noises, odors, and other senses. The ADHD brain is not very good at this. That extra information is not filtered out; it just keeps coming in, catching up on every detail and heaping one on top of another until the system is utterly overwhelmed.

ADHD and Emotional Sensitivities

ADHD emotions are frequently more intense, abrupt, and overwhelming. These heightened emotions subsequently flood and overwhelm the ADHD brain, causing people to act rashly and irrationally. But when you look at what is going on, it all makes sense.

It becomes a system under attack. Because the ADHD brain lacks an information filter, it is constantly bombarded with information, sensations, and environmental stimuli. This assault puts the body's sympathetic nerve system, or fight or flight alarm system, on high alert, ready to assist us in fighting off an attack, fleeing as quickly as possible, or freezing in the hope that an aggressor passes us by. On the other hand, this form of preparation leaves us viewing the world as though it were ready to harm us. As a result, any comment, passing glance, or missed remark is more than likely to be interpreted as something intended to hurt rather than unintentional or unrelated.

A Sponge of Emotions:

Furthermore, because the ADHD brain does not filter information, it is more likely to pick up every passing expression, every minute feature of a person's face. As a result, emotionally sensitive ADHD brains are extremely perceptive and a sponge of emotions. As a result, people with ADHD are often superb readers of other people's emotional states. They can nearly feel other people's emotions without being told. And, while this can be a valuable tool, it is also agonizing. It means that you are not only required to feel your feelings but are also vulnerable to the feelings of anyone else with whom you may come into contact.

In an instant, you can go from zero to sixty. The lack of a filter, which overwhelms the ADHD brain with sensations and other people's emotions, also makes it difficult to filter internal emotions. As a result, when an ADHD brain experiences a feeling, it experiences it at full force. ADHD brains do not regulate emotion (in the same way that they do not manage attention or action). They either feel things completely or not at all. It is not a dimmer switch but rather an on/off switch. So there is no such thing as "just a bit irritated"; the system swings from "I am all right" to full wrath in a second. When you combine this with a system under threat, the emotional disorders associated with ADHD begin to make sense.

Physical Sensitivities with ADHD

Because the ADHD brain lacks a filter, it is unable to adapt to sensations. Rather than perceiving an itchy tag in an item of clothing for a split second and then dismissing it, the ADHD brain never stops recognizing the tag. Instead, it spends the entire day attempting to focus on the vital things: your professor's lecture, your wife's grocery list, and your boss's most recent request. But the tag keeps resurfacing, and your attention has to ping-pong back and forth between the activity at hand and the itch at the back of your neck.

It is not only these sensations that keep popping into my head. It is also how deeply they are felt. That itchy sweater or the barking dog are not simply little annoyances; they are all-consuming, rage-inducing, sanity-stealing nightmares. Again, the ADHD brain's trouble with regulation comes into play here; these feelings are experienced to the maximum extent - it is not "just a little bothersome" or "just a little itchy". the ADHD brain does not just share the sensation, but it is overwhelmed by it.

How to Treat Hypersensitivity in ADHD

Hypersensitivity does not have a specific treatment. However, because it is caused partly by the ADHD brain's problem with regulation, any treatments that assist with ADHD brain control are also beneficial in reducing hypersensitivity.

Some examples:

ADHD medicine (both stimulant and non-stimulant): there is no hypersensitivity medication. However, ADHD medications help increase the brain's regulatory capacity, limiting how much it experiences something—both physically and emotionally. The drug also helps the brain focus where it needs to, tuning out what it needs to ignore the most.

Exercise: exercising is not just about losing weight and keeping your heart healthy. Many neurologists consider them joyful side effects of exercise's main purpose—keeping our brains at their best—which is especially true for ADHD brains. On a neurobiological level, physical exercise does the same (and more!) for the brain as ADHD medicine. More on the remarkable influence of exercise on the ADHD brain may be found here.

Meditation: as a practice, it has been shown to provide soothing and focused effects on the ADHD brain. This allows your system to return to a state of calm more quickly after becoming overwhelmed, and it also allows you to add some space before acting from an overwhelmed state.

Nutrition: keeping your body (and thus your brain) well-fed is critical for regulating emotions and feelings. Our brains consume 50% of our blood sugar, and without a regular supply, they cannot do the hard work of feeling just a tiny bit of a feeling or ignoring the car alarm down the street.

Sleep: getting 7-8 hours of quality sleep (not just before bed) nourishes your brain to its maximum natural capacity. Anything less than a full night's sleep begins to erode the body's ability to regulate.

Suggestions for living effectively with ADHD hypersensitivity

Increasing your brain's ability to regulate will not heal hypersensitivity, but it will only make it better and simpler to manage. So, if you cannot alter your brain, adjusting your environment is critical to living a fulfilling life.

Respect your brain: Recognize what works and what does not work for your brain. Do not make it do stuff. It is not good at.

Allow yourself space: If you become overwhelmed, take a break. Allow yourself some space from the things that are bothering you and center your thoughts. Then, after your system has calmed down, consider whether and how you want to re-engage.

<u>Block it out:</u> Use noise-canceling headphones, blue light blocking glasses, or other ways to block out all those extra stimuli.

<u>Set boundaries and expectations:</u> Once you have identified what overwhelms your brain, you may set boundaries to safeguard it. Do you have a buddy who has three boisterous children and two barking dogs? I recommend meeting at a park or for a girl's lunch. Do you get overwhelmed in busy places? Refuse to attend the large performance and instead agree to attend a modest outdoor event.

<u>Share it:</u> Telling others about your sensitivity will help them understand and respect your boundaries. Let them know how you feel (perhaps even share this article) and watch as views shift and compromises are found.

<u>Change things up.</u> Feeling overwhelmed by the massive superstore? Instead, go to your neighborhood supermarket. Can you not stand the tags? Commit to purchasing clothing with no tags. Do not subject your brain to the same amount of stimuli over and over; instead, start exploring ways to vary it.

Why do I become enraged about little matters?

70% of individuals with ADHD report having more frequent or strong rages than the general population. This makes sense at its core since the ADHD brain struggles with regulation. And it makes no distinction between which aspects of itself it struggles to manage. One of those things is anger. Rather than having a dimmer switch that enables only a small amount of fury, the ADHD brain turns its anger on/off switch and goes all in, being entirely flooded.

Overstimulation

Because the ADHD brain does not have a filter for irrelevant or extraneous information, it is under attack all day long, always absorbing an onslaught of extra stimulus. And, while this is the norm for the ADHD brain, it still feels like what it is: a nonstop barrage. This activates our basic fight/flight mechanism, prompting the brain to seek out any potential threats. This notice not only keeps us (at least theoretically) safe. It also has the added benefit of pulling us out of the uncomfortable state of anxiety/pain and into the more active (and thus less powerless, if not more comfortable) state of fury.

There are two forms of ADHD: poor management of anger and frustration. ADHD brains, as we all know, are a diverse bunch. Sure, there are some universal truths, but ADHD brains are as diverse and colorful as the wonderful people who possess them. As a result, researchers are always attempting to categorize ADHD brains to understand better (and treat) them. For example, according to one recent study, children with ADHD who struggle with aggression fall into two categories. (While this study did not include adults, I believe the ideas apply to adult ADHD brains as well.)

Irritable: People with ADHD who fall within this category are prone to rage. They are acutely aware of it on a regular and intense basis. They have difficulty getting over their anger, and they frequently dwell on the things that made them upset. In general, they experience more "negative" emotions (such as anger, impatience, frustration, despair, and hopelessness) than pleasant feelings (happiness, excitement, joy, etc.). As a result, they are prone to become trapped in negative cycles of aggravation, rage, and frustration.

Exuberant: People with ADHD experience a considerably broader spectrum of emotions, but they all feel them quite deeply. Their brains exhibit severe dysregulation and are extremely excitable. They are frequently sensation-seekers, looking for new adventures, and feel love and delight as profoundly as they do rage. Exuberant ADHDers experience brief bursts of anger, yet they let it go just as fast.

Anger vs. Frustration

We frequently mix up frustration and anger. They are connected, but they are not the same. Frustration is the feeling that emerges from barriers in our path—unmet needs, desires, or ambitions. Internal irritation frequently feels like a buildup of energy. I liken it to a horse at the starting gate: it wants to gallop and run quickly, but the barrier prevents him from displaying all that he has to offer.

ADHD minds are all too familiar with this sensation. Yet, in many respects, starting gate frustration is the fundamental challenge of the ADHD brain—the problem of turning intention into action.

The dissatisfied brain has two options. First, it can deflate and lose all of its steam and vitality when it is continually frustrating, a condition known as learned helplessness. So why bother when it appears like there is no point? The brain's alternative option for all that energy is to look for blame in your surroundings. When a flaw is discovered, there is a location for all of the frustration's pent-up energy to be released.

Frustration and rage: How to Handle anger?

Of course, it is preferable to avoid rage altogether. When we deal with it before it happens, we avoid having to deal with the dreaded emotion. ADHD brains have a harder time accomplishing this, but that is good because there is enough to do when you are upset or after an outburst. And the more you concentrate on whatever time frame is easy for you right now—before, during, or after—the others will begin to become easier as well.

Before the flare: I understand that planning or preparing for your rage is akin to arranging for a root canal: not only is it not ADHD-friendly but who wants to spend time thinking about or planning for such an unpleasant feeling? But bear with me because a little forethought at the onset can help you avoid several situations when your rage would otherwise take over.

Recognize your triggers: Is it your mother-in-subtle law's jabs every holiday that makes you want to scream, or is it rush hour that makes your hair stand on end? Next, consider the moments when you have become enraged; what are the common threads? These are the things that set you off. Having recognized them, you may begin to stop them in before they appear.

Manage your stimulation: If your system has already been overwhelmed with too much stimulus, you will be far more likely to tip the scales into anger. Manage your overstimulation and reduce your nervous system response to give your brain a greater chance of responding intelligently in the present.

Set your limits: because anger is a reaction to a threat, one of our largest triggers is someone breaking our emotional or physical boundaries. Understanding your boundaries and communicating them ahead of time might assist people in not crossing them.

Exercise: One of the reasons the ADHD brain suffers from anger is its inability to regulate itself. Exercise helps balance these regulatory difficulties by flooding the brain with the three happy brain musketeers: dopamine, serotonin, and norepinephrine. So, work up a sweat to give your brain the best chance of moderating the fury that comes it is away.

Sleep: Nothing says "angry" like a tired head. Cortisol floods our brains when we do not get enough sleep. Cortisol primes the brain to interpret everything around us as a threat, preventing us from thinking through events rationally. A good night's sleep nourishes our brains and turns off cortisol, allowing us to process information as efficiently as possible.

At the moment: When you are angry, the best thing you can do is make some space. This ensures that you do not injure anyone (or anything) around you and allows your emotions to move through you while your system settles down. How do you proceed to accomplish that goal, then? I use the abbreviation STOPP to help remind us of what we need most right now:

Space: Remove yourself (both physically and mentally) from the circumstance that is causing your rage.

Take a deep breath: Or two, or three can calm your body's reaction.

Observe: Are you aware of what's going on within yourself and around you? Remember that you are not in danger.

Your perspective: Now that your body is quiet and you have been reminded that you are fine, can you shed any light on what prompted your rage? What caused that person or object to act or say something that irritated you? What are the bigger picture variables at work?

Proceed: How can you proceed now that you have gained some perspective? What steps can you take to help fix the situation?

Following an outburst: Did you miss the triggers and find it difficult to move away? That is fine; everyone experiences this. You can still improve things-

Cleaning up and cleaning out: First and foremost, did you create chaos from your rage? Toss a plate, a load of laundry, or punch a hole in the wall? If this is the case, clean up the mess and mend any shattered pieces. Do not force yourself or your loved ones to endure the aftermath of the explosion again. When the cleanup is over, ask yourself, "Why did this happen?" What went wrong that caused this? Have you been overstimulated? Overtired? Have you been taking care of yourself? Do you need to set new or different limits?

Apologize: Now that you understand why and have gathered the physical components. It is time to reassemble the emotional puzzle. A genuine apology that accepts responsibility for acts is a unique gift that you may give to the world. And it is the start of the healing process. Every good apology consists of six parts:

- regret expression
- what went wrong is explained.
- acceptance of accountability
- repentance expression
- make an offer for substitution
- beg for forgiveness

Forgiveness: For the secondary feeling of anger to flare, you first identified someone to blame. Are you willing to forgive that individual for whatever they did? Yes? Great. The next stage is to forgive yourself. You went up in flames. You did not control your rage, and you may have caused some harm. But guess what? You are not by yourself. We have all done it—every single one of us. And you can be stronger for it if you have a decent plan, an honest apology, and a clear road forward.

The shame spiral

What exactly is the shame spiral? As an example, consider the following: "I am running late (feels a little guilty)...I am constantly late...everyone will notice...how can everyone else be doing great in life?...Why am I such a flop?....If I had simply tried harder...how come I did not wake up with the first alarm?...This is something that everyone else can do.

What is the matter with me?...I should remain at home...what is the purpose of going in if I am not going to be able to do it anyway?...I am going back to bed because I cannot do it."

Does this sound familiar? It is the negative thinking vortex spinning out of control. I hear some variation of this from my clients, my children, and my friends numerous times a day. It is universal, and we are all guilty of it. One little error kicks the bruise left by a lifetime of similar blunders, carrying with it the wall of humiliation left by a lifetime of criticism and self-blame. Because the embarrassment is so unbearable, individuals frequently turn away. They close their eyes, pull the blankets over their heads, and try to shut out the world and their thoughts.

This spiral is especially dangerous for the ADHD brain. For many, this is because even slight errors can set off a rejection-sensitive distress reaction. A history of previous failures is triggered, signaling a sense of shame, which leads to hopelessness, melancholy, and an often overpowering urge to hide from it all.

When we begin to have these thoughts, they activate negative feelings, which influence our behavior, We turn away from what is making us feel awful. We avoid it with whatever is brightest, shiniest, and most absorbing. For a short while, this works, but soon we understand what we are doing, and the consequences of avoiding that meeting, avoiding that paper, or skipping that quiz begin to sink in. This invokes a whole other set of terrible emotions and our numbed-out distraction is now invaded by feelings of shame, furthering the spiral.

This occurs as a result of the interconnectedness of our thoughts, feelings, and behaviors. When we adjust one, it affects the others. The

Cognitive Triangle is the interaction of thoughts, feelings, and behaviors. The connectivity of ideas, feelings, and behaviors may appear as terrible news in the shame spiral. When one falls, the others follow suit. But guess what? The other side is powerful and full of promise and possibility.

We can feel bad because of our negative ideas and avoidant behaviors. But what about good thoughts and behaviors? They make us happy. At the very least, they save us from feeling any worse. So now we have the key to reversing a downward spiral. Turning around a terrible day, or even just getting our day started on the right foot.

When we think positively (even about our failures), our moods shift from hopeless to hopeful, and we feel more capable and in control. Then, as an example, we can address the issues that need to be addressed to solve the problem.

The real-world application of thinking power:

Contrast the following these mental patterns:

"I do not have the time for this...

"I cannot believe I waited so long...what was the point of all that work I would be putting on myself..."

"It will be a nightmare, and everyone will know I don't have what it takes..."

"I cannot deal with this."

"Wow. I do not have much time...I wish I had started sooner."

"Okay, next time, I will try to figure out how to start earlier, but this time? Let's see: what do I need to do? What exact amount of time do I have? Is there any wriggle room for me?...Okay, I will do it. Let us get started!"

Just writing the these makes me want to crawl back under the covers. What about the second? That one has hope, a plan, and a sense of calm certainty. The person holding those thoughts is likely to begin; they may not complete the job or at least not as well as they would have desired, but they are likely to complete a large proportion and may find a way to make it sufficient.

What else is there to say? The second is much more likely to result in some modified habits to ensure that this pattern does not repeat itself the next time because they did not throw up their hands and swear they could never do it. In essence, they treated it as if it were "figureoutable," in the words of Marie Forleo.

Changing one's mind, while a simple concept, is a difficult task. It requires deliberate effort, and it does not always feel authentic. But you know what is cool? It does not even have to be completely correct to affect your emotions. Even if you tell yourself, "It is okay, I know I am trying, I will figure it out," and it seems hollow? That is fine—first and foremost, the more you repeat it, the stronger it will feel; second, even a false comfort can stop a shame spiral.

The Influence of Behavior

However, changing your thoughts is not your only option. Behaviors are also effective. Do you have a negative self-image? Sure, the instinct is to get as far away from such feelings as possible. TV, the internet, social media, shopping, sex, and drink are all bright and dazzling numbing agents. They allow us to become absorbed in something for long enough to provide us with a brief respite. The trouble with them is that they usually do not give much fuel, so we return to the original situation, now with less time and even fewer resources to cope.

Fuel stops, on the other hand, provide us with the space to gain clarity while simultaneously providing us with the resources to handle the issue. So what can you do for yourself (or someone else) that will keep you going? Perhaps you can take a quick walk around the block, phone a friend, prepare a meal for a homeless shelter, pay a visit to your grandma, work on a creative project, or play with your kids on the floor. All of these things provide both perspectives and fuel.

I understand that it is not easy to DO stuff when you are feeling down. Our ADHD brain has been crawling through a puddle of humiliation, draining all the energy your brain had, and now a walk around the block may be equivalent to a brisk race up Mt Everest. That means it is even more important to use your ADHD techniques, such as telling yourself you only need to take two steps (breaking the work down), inviting a friend to join you for a walk (accountability), or making your stroll conclude at your favorite juice bar (using reward).

All of these tasks will be easier if you plan ahead. When you are in a poor mood, it is not easy to think of positive things to do. It is like trying to think of something healthy to eat when you are hungry; the donut seems far more delicious. So, in these awful places, give yourself the benefit of a pre-made menu from which to choose. What behaviors might you engage in that will provide you with both perspective and fuel when you are in a shame spiral? Struggle to come up with a few that fit a variety of scenarios and time constraints such as short, some that are longer, some that involve people, and others that you can do alone, some that demand physical activity and some that can be done sat. This way, you will have options for almost every situation.

So, the next time you are feeling down, remember this. Examine what your ideas and actions were doing. Were you on a downward spiral? Give yourself a mental embrace as I did for my son. Speak gently and sweetly to yourself, and then go over your list to see what you can DO to nourish yourself and your viewpoint. You can flip that spiral around at any time. Is it difficult? Yes. But you are capable of overcoming adversity.

Rejection Sensitive Dysphoria (RSD)

Do you know how it feels like someone strapped you into an emotional rollercoaster without your consent? The idea that you can have everything lined up for a fantastic day—sleep, exercise, a solid plan— but one event can send your emotions into a tailspin and toss it all out the window? Do you ever wonder why you are so depressed?

If this is the case, you are not alone. You could be suffering from Rejection Sensitive Dysphoria, a condition about which psychologists are still studying. However, there is growing consensus on what it is, who is most likely to have trouble with it, and what can be done to address it. So let us get started:

Rejection Sensitive Dysphoria (RSD) is a condition that causes feelings of rejection. RSD is characterized by excessive emotional sensitivity and suffering in response to perceived failure, rejection, projection of potential loss, or criticism.

When faced with rejection, people with RSD experience intense agony, rage, or depression. The real kicker here is that it does not have to be an actual rejection. It could be the fear of rejection or even the mere possibility that they would be rejected. The same is true of failure: sentiments of failure can arise even when someone does not believe that failure is a possibility.

What causes RSD?

It is frequently simpler to grasp RSD when it is sparked by true failure or rejection. For example, if someone with RSD performs poorly on a large project, he or she will not get promoted. This elicits a strong emotional response. It is excruciatingly uncomfortable, yet it makes perfect sense. However, because RSD can be triggered by potential, perceived, or even imagined failure or rejection, it is not always straightforward.

Looking at a task list consisting of demanding projects and objects, as well as thoughts like "I'll never be able to complete this." or "I know I am not going to be able to get this done, why do I even try," can set off an RSD reaction. An accidental slight from a buddy can set it off. It can be caused by a fear of failure or even inadvertent criticism such as "why do not you just set the alarm, so you are not constantly late?"

How does Rejection Sensitivity Dysphoria appear?

There is a spectrum of RSD reactions. As a result, they can be minor melancholy, frustration, or discontent. They can, however, be as severe as a full-fledged depressive episode, complete with suicide thoughts, excessive rage, hopelessness, or extreme social isolation. These feelings can be directed either against oneself or at someone else.

RSD that is internalized: When a person internalizes his RSD reaction, it resembles depression. Internalized RSD is typically characterized by melancholy, hopelessness, self-blame, and self-hatred. "I am such a failure," "I never do anything right," or "I am so foolish" are common phrases. It appears to be sitting on the couch, hiding under the covers, procrastinating, or seeking distraction.

RSD that has been externalized: Externalized RSD reactions are aimed against people or things other than yourself. They are typically characterized by sentiments of rage, severe exasperation, and resentment. Externalized RSD reactions might take the form of ranting, tantrums, violence or calm simmering, passive-aggressiveness, or even determined competitiveness. Externalized RSD reactions frequently feel explosive and as though they appear out of nowhere.

When a person with RSD also has ADHD, these feelings have a significant influence on productivity. For example, when you look at your task list, you could feel overwhelmed and distracted, and you might imagine that you will not be able to do everything. This produces the pain and agitation of RSD, which leads to additional avoidance and procrastination, which reinforces your idea that you cannot do it and worsens your sentiments. (For more detail on this negative spiral and how to break free, see The Shame Spiral page.)

How can I tell whether I have Rejection Sensitive Dysphoria?

Because RSD can induce such intense emotions, it is occasionally misdiagnosed as bipolar disease, borderline personality disorder, or social anxiety disorder. The essential difference, though, is what causes the feelings. If the surfaces are provoked exclusively by failure, rejection, or criticism and are swiftly reversed by success, acceptance, or production, RSD is most likely to blame.

Because we are still learning about RSD and it is not yet included in the Diagnostic and Statistical Manual (DSM-5) we do not have all of the prerequisites for it.

What is the relationship between RSD and ADHD? We suspect that those with ADHD (as well as autism) are more likely to get RSD. We do not know why, but it appears to be related to the fact that ADHD patients have hypersensitive nerve systems. Of course, not everyone with ADHD has RSD, but if you have ADHD, you are more likely to battle rejection hypersensitivity.

Nobody enjoys being rejected. Nobody likes being criticized. We must be part of a group as humans; our lives depends on it. As a result, our brains are hardwired to want connection and despise rejection. Our brains are also constructed to be hyperaware of and retain any indication that we have made a mistake. This, too, protects us. We can do better the next time if we know where we went wrong.

However, the ADHD brain is particularly prone to and sensitive to this sensation. I frequently discuss how the ADHD brain lacks a filter for what it encounters. Therefore, it cannot keep the unimportant out. However, it has a difficult time letting go of things that look out of place or are bothersome (like that itchy tag at the back of your shirt). These two ADHD brain tendencies may prevent it from being able to keep rejection under check. It cannot filter out, so it retains it until it has made total sense of it and is no longer annoying.

So, I have been diagnosed with RSD; what should I do now? To begin with, you are not alone, and you are not exaggerating your emotions. However, because of the way your brain is constructed, this discomfort is flooding it. Beating yourself up over it, feeling guilty and ashamed, will only make matters worse.

There is some indication that drugs like Guanfacine (originally used to treat high blood pressure) can help with RSD symptoms. If you have severe rejection sensitivity, you should discuss a trial run with your psychiatrist. Medication for RSD is excellent because the symptoms can occur unexpectedly. On the other hand, medication may not help for every rejection, and it may not be a practical option for everyone. As a result, dealing with the thoughts associated with the feelings as they arise is an important next step. Here are some approaches for dealing with those thoughts when they arise:

Recognize your patterns: do you ever feel unwelcome at parties? Do you ever feel excluded in a group of three?? Is an excessively extensive job list leaving you feeling overwhelmed and depressed in the face of certain failure? Do you get shaken up by constructive criticism? Make a list of the last five times you were rejected, or your RSD was triggered. Is there anything that stands out? Knowing where you are prone to these feelings will help you overcome them more quickly.

Thought charting: Writing down what happened, how you felt about it, what it triggered in you, and then the evidence for and against your interpretation might help you bring your logical brain back into the equation and calm the rejection.

The STOPP method: make some room, Take a deep breath, observe, put things into perspective, and then go on. It is a tried-and-true CBT strategy for dealing with overwhelming emotions and not reacting with your feelings rather than your logical intellect.

Exercise: A quick walk, fast jog with music blasting, kickboxing class, or other high-intensity cardio might help burn off the excess energy and aggressiveness caused by criticism or rejection. After you have burned it off, you might find it easier to talk yourself through the experience.

Improve your self-talk: Talking to yourself as though you were a kind, sympathetic coach or a loving, wise grandmother can help you cope with rejection. Every successful self-talk session covers three topics:

Validation of your emotions

Perspective enlargement (what else could be at work that your initial feelings and assumptions may have overlooked?)

Steps to follow (what are you going to do now to help)

Meditation: A meditation practice can help you become more aware of your thought processes, improve your capacity to let go of thoughts that are no longer useful to you, and strengthen your general connection to thoughts.

Perspective-taking: Because RSD is frequently a reaction to imagined or perceived criticism or rejection, having a different point of view might be crucial in addressing the upset. You may ask a friend or spouse for their opinion or consider other perspectives a caring and loving friend could provide you. In any case, attempt to come up with at least three different explanations for the situation and then choose the one that makes the most sense.

Chapter 15:
The Power of Encouragement and ADHD

T he power of encouragement is one of my favorite topics because who does not want to be encouraged by their partner? Suppose you are riding your bicycles and your partner is a much better cyclist than you. He encourages you by saying, "You have gotten so much stronger and you are really doing well today. I am having trouble keeping up with you."

You have to admit that it is a sort of cynical response. Still, you will be quite pleased that he sees those things. You will be thinking, "This is the motivation I have been looking for. I have to keep doing this." How relevant is this for couples looking to encourage each other and improve their relationship? It takes encouragement, unlike the other day-to-day stuff. Effort is required in a relationship and like daily love notes with beautiful remarks? One of the most important types of communication that an ADHD partner can offer to a non-ADHD partner is fully engaging with managing their ADHD. It communicates something very specific, which is, "I care about you. I care about us, and I really want to work on my part conversely".

The same thing you get from an ADHD partner is thinking about all the things they can do to make their contribution better, whether about parenting, being more composed or less angry, or treating your partner with respect. Then comes determination when the other person notices. One of the issues for non-ADHD partners is that sometimes they are afraid to tell their ADHD partner that they have noticed everything and want to encourage them. But then they think if they do encourage them, their partner will essentially go into rest mode and stop doing the work they are doing.

If they withhold it, you know there is slight punishing or a force pushing the partner. That is the wrong approach because people are much more motivated by encouragement through acknowledgment than by being punished or having affection withheld. Eventually, if affection is withheld, the response will be, "It does not matter what I do since my partner never notices anyway. Why should I bother trying."

There was a couple where the female did not have ADHD; She liked to niggle or cuddle on the couch. The person with ADHD had hyperactivity and could not sit still for anything - I mean for anything. Still, his partner expressed how much she likes this, so we came up with a diabolical plan. The next time it was going to rain, he would go for a 15-mile run, come home, get his wife. They were going to watch something on Netflix. He goes upstairs and takes a shower and they get on the couch. He a cover and promptly cuddles up with her and falls asleep. A couple of days later, it is a little bit different. Still, it was an interesting coaching call because his wife called me one day and asked, "have you guys talked about it?"

I said yes, that was our plan. The idea was for him to get so tired that he could sit there and meet her in his arms. She started to weep at that because she realized how difficult it was for him, yet it was all intentional. It was interesting because it provided some motivation for him. After all, he realized that they came together despite how hard it was. It was really a big deal for her. She felt good that he had tried and then he felt good about it. It made her cry. I am also happy that they could connect because I thought there is a meeting in the middle that would happen for them. Maybe the tears were of joy because she realized he was coming from his heart and trying hard. It was not direct encouragement but it worked. The response symptom made him feel encouraged. When she acknowledged that he was even more motivated to do cuddle, the symptom response increased.

It is almost impossible to motivate a person who has ADHD with potential punishment. It just does not work because of the wiring the neurochemistry of the ADHD brain, which is very reward focused. It is not punishment focused; it is not about consequences. If you think about it, you may say you know why your partner does not ever remember the consequences of past actions because you seek to reward. This support is really important, and it is not about faking it. It is not about saying thank you: it is about genuinely saying, wow, this is hard for my partner and she acknowledged effort.

It was not great that he fell asleep so particular approach did not work perfectly. I have heard of people falling asleep as soon as they get comfy. On the other hand, it gives them an entree to deal with it. It does not come naturally but it is still a good foundation to build a really strong relationship if you do it regularly. Everybody wants a great relationship. Here encouragement is really important. It is incredibly motivating and to be seen and appreciated by your partner.

Sometimes I say to non-ADHD partners, make sure to say thank you, and their response is, "why should I say thank you if my partner is doing something they ought to be doing anyway." My point is twofold: first you are a nice person. It is a nice thing to do, and second because it is much harder for your partner to do something that is not interesting than it is for you to do it. It is always good to let them know that that effort is well taken.

Chapter 16:
Making ADHD your superpower

Y es, you can be smart and successful and still struggle with ADHD. My favorite rule is never to worry alone. This chapters is designed to help you overcome the number one challenge holding you back: a lack of belief in yourself. Let's live our best belief lives and learn how to make ADHD a superpower.

There is a study by scientists who study genetics. They found that the three main traits of ADHD are impulsivity, risk-taking, and constant novelty seeking (finding new ways to do something when you do not need to) and stopping projects and starting new ones. These same three traits are tied to a genetic mutation that inhibits the production of dopamine, the feel-good chemical. So, for people with ADHD to feel good, they need stimulation. If they do not find stimulation out there, they will cause the stimulation: They will fight. They will draw extremely long penalties in hockey games. They will skateboard, they will snowboard, and go to punk rock concerts in the dangerous parts of Pittsburgh every Friday and Saturday night for six years in a row.

It may be just to feel normal or feel good. The same scientists also found out that this gene mutation has been positively selected since time immemorial. That means that whenever one of our caveman brothers or sisters exhibited those same three traits of impulsivity, risk-taking ingenuity, they were capable of doing greater things. This is usually seen when people with ADHD in a crowd sit up a little prouder and feel less ashamed. But why is that? What do these three traits have to do with passing on a gene?

Think about it. They are in the same tribe or clan of cave people. It is nighttime. They are sitting out in front of the cave before a fire. Beyond what they can see, there is a very slight snap of a twig. They will rise with their spears and plunge into danger without thinking of the safety of their tribe and its families. And when they return to the tribe, they are saved and mate with their partners. This is certain a phenomenon if saber-toothed tigers are hunting them down!

But how does a survival mechanism in the Stone Age turn it into a success mechanism in the 21st century? You do it by purposefully engaging the fight or flight response in people with ADHD. Our nervous system is primed to live with our heads on a pivot and constantly look for that saber-toothed tiger because we are ready. And when it happens, we are at our best. In short, when things are at their worst, we do better.

So how do they bring this fight or flight response about? The better question is, when do they bring this fight or flight response about? They bring at the moment of overwhelm. Everybody experiences overwhelm at some point in life. But people with ADHD experience overwhelm multiple times a day. Their brains work so fast and they have a billion ideas flowing at once. They have immense physical energy amid chaos except there are not enough outlets for all the energy. Then all of a sudden, there is a shutdown.

A shutdown is what kills relationships and careers for people with ADHD. There is that moment before the shutdown, though, where it feels like the world is collapsing in on them. You want to run away from whatever it is you are doing that is overwhelming. You can do a very simple exercise called a brain dump when you start to feel a tightening your chest. You feel like the world's collapsing around you.

You crack open a notebook, put pen to paper, and start writing. It does not need to be legible to anybody; it just needs to be grammatically correct. It could be thoughts or random words. It could be an entire sentence. It could be doodles. It could be whatever as it comes into your head onto the page. Something amazing is going to happen. You have been impulsive, and you have allotted time to self-control. You have engaged in fight or flight and jumped into the darkness, facing the spirit of a saber-toothed tiger. This feeling is what people experience after they get in a fight. After they disrupt the class or meeting, it allows them to take all those ideas they had swirling and coming at them at lightning speed. With the exercise, they can prioritizing and move on.

The real superpower with ADHD is learning to balance the two sides of this gift. You have to know when to go into fight or flight so you can use those ideas and work with people - mundane things like balancing the books. You know when you need to take your hands off the wheel and become a bit impulsive, a little reckless and take risks. Everybody with ADHD needs to master this ability. It is not good enough that the fight or flight response saved the human race because the human race is facing a lot of big problems right now. The only way out of it for them is with impulsivity, risk-taking, and ingenuity. But it is counterproductive, of course.

If you have ADHD and been told by your parents and teachers or doctor that you are never going to be successful, you will have a hard time living your daily life. I am here to tell you that they are wrong. It is the big fat lie. It is about time that you find out that if you have ADHD, you are not disabled. Actually, you have a superpower, and if you know how to use it, you will be able to use it. And you will be successful in anything you are doing.

ADHD is definitely not a disability.

It is just how some of us are if we understand how our brain works and how we need to manage everything on a day-to-day basis to be successful. We can even surpass a lot of people around us because we have some really crazy superpower that a lot of people do not. As you know, there are three types of ADHD with different consequences. Number one is that impulsive and hyperactive children have very typical behavior in school, especially boys. they are going to be running around all day, and they cannot sit up straight. They always must be doing something really interesting and fun to keep their dopamine level up.

This type of ADHD is a very common and easily diagnosed because a lot of teachers or parents who are close to these kids notice the behavior right away. The second type includes inattentive people who cannot really focus, especially on the things they do not like to do. Sometimes these students are sitting in class and they pay no attention to what is going on in class. They might be doing their own thing or are bored. The third type is a combination of both. It depends on the situation and environment.

Image you are a person with ADHD and are facing difficulty in math and science. To maintain passing grades, you have to work with double the effort than normal. On the other hand, you will likely figure out very efficient ways to study. So if that is something you struggle with, it is all about taking notes and using a system to stay organized. You will want to review how many hours you have to put into studying.

If you want to be successful at something, just because you have ADHD does not mean that you cannot achieve it. Even if you want to get a degree in astrophysics, you can follow these steps and work even harder to get there. You can overcome the struggle with your working memory and forgetting everything. Work harder if you really need to do something exciting like passing a calculus course.

But if you do not love what you are doing and have tried and practice, but you cannot get there, your only option is to work even harder than every single one of your classmates. You have to do every single math problem and follow every single worksheet to be able to do well in the course. But there is no excuse. If you really have to do something, you have to find a way.

For success, the most important thing is to love what you are doing. How do you do that? How do you love something? How do you know you love something? the only way to find out that you love something is to try new things. Once you try new things, take on new activities, you will find out what you like spend time to become really, really good.

Once you become really, really good at something, then you start loving it. You are not going to love it right away, especially all the things worth pursuing. If you started trying some new, you had to learn new skills too. Initially, it will be very confusing. It will be overwhelming. And it seems like a lot of work. But when you start getting into it and really improving on your skills, you will realize that you are really good at it.

You will become really excited and in love with the process. With time you will become super focused and in love with it. That is the incredible power of ADHD. If you have ADHD, you will be super focused on the things you love. But you will not know that you love the process if you do not start it. I really recommend trying new things, even though it may seem very overwhelming and confusing at first.

People with ADHD also struggle with weight loss. They really struggle with keeping their weight down and binge eating. People who have ADHD really struggle because they try to get their dopamine from a lot of negative activities. And as they become older and less active, they try to get this dopamine from carbs and sugar. They become overweight because by binge. Sticking to a restricted or healthy diet is an excessively big challenge for them.

I can't express enough how critical it is to work on your health. You will see a significant change when you start paying more attention to yourself. That includes exercising, dieting, sleeping on time, meditating, yoga, and stretching, among other valuable practices. These five things are important in your life because they will help your ADHD the most. A vast number of research studies on the benefits of exercise and nutrition for people with ADHD have been conducted. So if you feel like your nutrition and health could improve, do not do it just because of your health. Do it for your ADHD because life becomes so much easier and more interesting way.

I will try to tell you how to pick the right career and activities for you. Because we are all unique, there are a few things to keep in mind. How do we find the careers best for people with ADHD? If you are a passionate person, you really like people and really like helping them. If you feel like it something you could relate to, you can consider being a social worker. Consider following a high-intensity career. If you are a person who is always on the go and want to do exciting and new things all the time, you could really consider becoming a detective, police officer, nurse, correctional officer, emergency dispatcher, sports coach, a firefighter or any other career keeps your dopamine level up during the day.

We are prone to become extremely worried and overwhelmed. So we have to make sure that we do meditation activities such as yoga and stretching, especially before asleep. There are those people who are actually creative and are able look at things from a different and personal view. They always stand out. They can chose a career as an artist, designer, architect, or anything that involves creativity.

Another group of people get a lot of ideas during the day, and they act on them. They get really, really excited about an idea. They want to do it and right away. this is something most people struggle with ADHD or not. Some people get an idea, and then before they start doing something about it, they talk themselves out of it. ADHD people are going to do it right away no matter what. It could be as mundane as finishing a whole Nutella jar by themselves, and they will do it. That is the negative part of the condition. But if you get an idea to start a business and want to run all the way at it, they will also do it and flourish. In the end, you decide how you want to use your superpower. You can use it to maintain your ideal or to become successful in business.

People with ADHD can improve their working memory if they start teaching others. They will notice that they can hold onto information a lot longer than they did before. It becomes so much easier for them to communicate what they need to convey and so much to remember their appointments and such that because they have become healthier. Teaching can play a huge role here.

Socially, people with ADHD are used to focusing on negativities. And after started doing all this new healthy stuff and doing the things they love, they really do not have to struggle so much anymore. They will be able to stay positive, radiant and loving towards everyone around them as opposed to before.

If you are a spouse of a person with ADHD, you should know by now that there is light at the end of the tunnel. The vast majority of literature has cited a variety of good features that ADHD has contributed to relationships. The most common characteristic is spontaneity.

"My spouse adores my spontaneous, never-say-die attitude," an ADHD woman explained. "He is astounded by how productive I am when hyperfocus kicks in and by how accepting I am of others who struggle."

Hyperfocus was cited as both a positive and negative aspect ("My hyper-focus on him when we were dating resulted in our marriage, but after we had children, I hyper-focused on them, which made him feel I did not love him.") and as a positive and good influence ("Using my hyperfocus to our benefit when I work hard is a skill I have developed.").

Creativity is rated highly as a favorable characteristic in a marriage partner with ADHD. Respondents to surveys in studies agree that creativity adds excitement to everyday life, making for exceptional occasions.

For example, "I am fantastic at parties!" "I try to make every event as personal and considerate as possible, and I am quite creative," said an ADHD wife.

Chapter 17:
The Role of Unconscious Shame in ADHD Symptoms

M any of you - and maybe even most of you - consider psychoanalysis to be an outdated, outmoded form of treatment. I have departed dramatically from the way I was trained. All the same, I believe that a lot of what psychoanalysts have observed and written about in the last 100 years is still relevant to an understanding of the unconscious processes in ADHD. I do not mean that researchers are now offering a new theory about ADHD that applies across the board. But I would like to share my experience working with several people who fit the profile and whose distractibility, poor impulse control, and difficulty in focusing attention have roots in unconscious pain.

These days, in the psych literature, it seems that talking about the unconscious mind has gone out of favor. The predominant treatment approaches are, of course, pharmacological and cognitive-behavioral, while the idea of searching for the unconscious roots of symptoms seems almost odd. It has become a part of our belief system and at the same time it has penetrated the mainstream culture.

Since Freud began writing about it more than a century ago, the psychoanalytic view that there are aspects of ourselves of which we're not conscious has gone mainstream. Take, for one example, the so-called Freudian slip. Most of us have examples from our personal lives, and Freudian slips are a staple of Hollywood movies from Annie Hall to Liar Liar.

Psychological defense mechanisms keep us from knowing parts of ourselves, of course. And even if psychologists do not write much about them these days, a collective belief in the existence of defense has also entered the mainstream. We often talk about a person behaving defensively, or we refer to someone as repressed.

Have you ever described a person as in denial, or have you told someone to stop projecting? These all reflect psychoanalytic concepts that have been absorbed into the cultural mainstream.

We are saddled with a lot of bad English translations of Freud's work, and defense mechanisms are one of them. A better translation of Freud's words in German would be warding off or fending off. One climbing analyst has defined psychological defense mechanisms as lies we tell ourselves to evade pain. So, in other words, we fend off or ward off the truths we find too painful to bear, excluding them from conscious awareness and isolating them in the unconscious.

In recent years, I have come to think of a defense mechanism as a shift of attention away from pain so you do not have to notice it. Do not pay attention to that painful emotion. Focus on this other thought or feeling instead. Sometimes I think of defenses working how a magician operates by effectively distracting you from what you are not supposed to notice. We refer to the unnoticed thought or feeling as unconscious, but it is still waiting to be noticed.

By the way, Wilfred Beyond's theories about truth and lying and psychotic attacks on the ability to pay attention have deeply influenced me. Now, in my work with people with ADHD who might be described as overly cerebral, I usually educate them about their feelings. Although the process occurs automatically for most of us, we know what we feel by observing sensations in specific areas of our bodies. I know I am sad, for example, by sensations arising in my eyes, throat, and chest.

If you live in your head, caught up in endless verbal thoughts, then you might never notice what you feel because you are not paying attention to your body. The feeling remains unconscious, unnoticed.

Distracting your attention and yourself from pain is sometimes an adaptive response and a very useful skill to have in your toolbox. Here is one of my favorite examples from popular culture: in Gone with the Wind Scarlett O'Hara says," I will not think about it. Now. I will think about it tomorrow when I can stand it." Scarlett is one of the great survivors in film and literature. And much of her strength comes from this ability to ignore pain, loss, hunger, disappointment, and so forth and do what needs to be done. By shifting into action mode, she distracts herself from what she cannot bear to feel is a big part of her strength.

It is also easy to become overly reliant on distraction as a means of coping with immense pain. In the remainder of my discussion, I'll discuss several different people with ADHD who I've worked with over the years, all of whom came to me with a prior ADHD diagnosis. They did not come to me specifically for help with that issue. I do not treat people for specific orders, and I do not subscribe to the current disease model of mental health that dominates our profession. But in my work with people with ADHD, we came to understand how unconscious pain and defenses against it play a role in ADHD symptoms.

Dana was one of these people with ADHD. She wanted to work with an online therapist because her job required her to travel for months at a time, and going to a therapist's office consistently was impossible. She was in her mid-20s. At the time we began working together, she was an attractive, intelligent young woman who had struggled with procrastination for most of her life and an inability to follow through on school and work-related tasks. Dana had been conceived when her mother had an extramarital affair with a man who was HIV positive. Dana herself was born HIV positive and has been on antivirals her entire life. As a result of that affair, her parents divorced during her first year of life, and her father remarried. Not long after, from an early age. Dana recalls feeling like there was something wrong with her. One of her earliest memories is of her stepmother. She forces her to wear surgical gloves and kept her at arm's length literally and figuratively. Her biological mother fell into a deep depression following the divorce and subsequently led a chaotic, financially unstable life. For Dana, physical affection and the experience of bringing joy to her parents were largely absent from her life.

So when I talk about core shame, or an experience of feeling damaged, ugly, defective, inferior, it takes root in the earliest months and years of life and results from failures of attachment, where joy is largely absent. It is usually - but not always - an unconscious experience. And we defend against the awareness of it in various ways.

Dana warded off feelings of profound shame by running away from or distracting herself from therapy. She developed a sort of false anti-shame self that was intended to disprove her feelings of shame. But, unfortunately, this new and improved Dana tended to be a bit grandiose, with a drive toward achievement in more areas than humanly possible. Music, athletic, academics: she tried to excel in too many areas and mastered none.

Whenever she felt frustrated, she would shift away from whatever activity she was engaged in and move on to another. It happened whenever she encountered a shameful experience caused by not performing as well as expected. Because she had not managed to practice or study enough, she would usually abandon the endeavor altogether and take up a different instrument to pursue a different sport. As she grew older and began dating, she had many short-term relationships that fell apart because she could not find a way to tell her partners about her HIV status, a source of great shame to her, although she intellectually understood that it was not her fault. In her mid-20s, when she finally did become more honest, she was met with consistent and humiliating rejection from men, terrified that she would infect them.

Her work together focused on helping Dana learn to face and bear with her shame rather than running away or distracting herself from it. When shame and distractibility are an issue, you will often have to deal with missed or forgotten sessions, and the additional shame stirs up. Dana often forgot her sessions. She would later send me an apology and then disappear from treatment for a month or two. Then, after she had recovered from the shame of forgetting, she would get back in touch.

I finally decided to send Dana reminders about our sessions on the day before. I would send a brief email confirming tomorrow's session at 8 a.m. she needed my help in remembering. Usually, I do not send reminders to most people with ADHD, but I wanted to help Dana avoid situations that would stir up even more shame.

This combination of core shame and defensive grandiosity has come up with another client I have worked with for several years now. Mark is an entrepreneur, one of the most creative business people I have ever known and very successful despite his distractibility and difficulty staying focused. I have been in session with Mark when he would discuss something in his business, and he suddenly would have several extremely creative ideas about ways to expand one after the other. He would eventually wind up losing focus. Like Dana, Mark tries to do too many things at once and works for too many hours every day, in part because he is not able to focus and become more efficient.

Mark originally came to me because, during long drives between home and his remote people with ADHD, he found himself breaking down and sobbing for no reason he could understand. Mark most definitely lives in his head. Helping him move down into his body and pay attention to his pain has been a lengthy process. Whenever difficult emotion enters the field, he tends to jump away from it.

Throughout our work together, we have uncovered unconscious shame with roots in his early childhood, a mother whom he describes as ruthless, and the father so addicted to pain pills that he pulled his own teeth out to get physicians to renew his prescriptions.

Alan, an online securities trader, came to me because he had become paralyzed following some large trading losses and could no longer function in his job. Completing a financial analysis and deciding upon a trade came easily to him. However, when it came time to act, he was unable to pull the trigger. As he put it, he wound up distracting himself with online games or household chores - anything to avoid having to follow through on a decision. As a child, he had had many behavior problems at school, largely because of poor impulse control. In our work together, the story did not end well. Alan revealed that he had always felt like a loser.

When core shame is an issue, the language of winners and losers often comes up, which is a major hint. On some level, being a loser means being ugly, defective, damaged, or inferior. I was able to help Alan recognize that his recent trading losses had stirred up his dread of being a loser and that he would do anything else rather than risk further exposure to shame. After five or six sessions, we decided to try a real-time experiment. During our next session, I would be present while he attempted to execute a trade. He is ready to do his research in advance and come prepared to follow a stock's fluctuation and ready to pull the trigger. When his models told him, the time was ripe.

He did not show up at our next session, and he failed to respond to my subsequent emails. I never heard from him again. I learned from this experience that successfully facing shame within a therapy session takes a strong bond between a therapist and client. Although I cannot be sure, I believe that the prospect of me present to witness him stirred up unbearable dread.

Since then, I have tried this experiment with another client, one I have worked with for several years. Nigel and I have developed a strong bond of respect and affection over the years. And by the way, one thing I have noticed during my career is that I find endearing my most successful people with ADHD. And it is not just the people with ADHD who strike me that way - with the most powerful connection I ever felt. The most meaningful work I have done during my career was with a young woman who displayed powerful symptoms of borderline personality disorder.

I found Nigel very endearing despite a somewhat pugnacious personality that had gotten him into trouble over the years. He had seen several therapists already during his 20s and received many different diagnoses: major depression, bipolar disorder, ADHD, and most recently, narcissistic personality disorder.

Nigel came from a high functioning family with two Ph.D. parents, but his childhood was characterized by pervasive anxiety. He described his parents as remote, argumentative, and preoccupied obsessively with their own worries, to such a degree that he constantly felt flooded and overwhelmed. He dreaded bringing friends home because his parents' nonstop bickering seems so dysfunctional. He recalled feeling weird from an early age, like an outsider and not liked by the other kids. At the same time, he had done extremely well academically up through high school. I think largely because he was so brilliant that everything came easily to him.

However, he had a cocky, overly confident air about him, which eventually got him into trouble. After earning his MBA from a prestigious business school, he worked in-house for two investment banks and lost both jobs because of a rebellious attitude. Because of procrastination, an inability to follow through, and eventually being unable to get out of bed in time for work. Nigel's superior and aggressive personality, a defense against core shame, did not help.

When we first began working together, Nigel was in the process of starting an online business. The challenges involved confronted him with many opportunities to experience shame, all of them revolving around rejection and interpersonal relationships. If he needed to reach out to an angel for funding, he would dread the prospect of being turned down so powerfully that he would not send the emails or make the necessary calls. Likewise, if he needed to hire someone new for his team, he would repeatedly reschedule interviews because he was afraid that he would not come across as confident to the potential recruit and they would not want to work for him.

During his workday, he would constantly shift between one task and another, never completing any of them. He would work on one sentence or one paragraph for hours, or he disappeared down the Wikipedia rabbit hole, as he called it. Research on one topic led him to another and another and another, ad infinitum. Oversleeping and missing his early morning sessions was an issue for Nigel, as it had been for Dana. Sleep was the ultimate defense against perspective shame and severely impeded his progress in his business and therapy. I settled on the same email reminder strategy with Nigel, but it was less effective because he would still sleep through his session upon occasion. However, he did not disappear from treatment.

Nigel eventually abandoned his startup and began applying for jobs. The same issues of distraction, procrastination, and excessive sleeping cropped up. When he began having trouble completing job applications, I suggested the same experiment I had wanted to try with Alan. We agreed that in our next session, I would be present while he reviewed and applied online. I believe my presence helped him focus, and it turned out to be "not so terribly anxiety-producing." He was able to complete it successfully. On this occasion and throughout my recent work with Alan, I have expressed my joy in seeing him succeed.

I find this to be crucial in helping people with ADHD heal from shame. He did not experience a joyful, securely attached parent. A joyful, fully engaged therapist is only second best, but it is what I have to offer. My joy was sincerely felt, I should say, and I believed that simulating such feelings would be ineffective. I believe in Nigel if I can put it that way. I am sincerely happy and proud of him when he succeeds. We have tried this approach on several occasions, some more successful than others. But I believe he is getting stronger, more shame resilient, and less frightened by the prospect of future encounters with shame. At the same time, the ADHD-like symptoms, distractibility, impulsiveness, procrastination have waned in intensity; now he is better able to concentrate and complete tasks in less time, and he is growing more confident in his own abilities and becoming a less pugnacious and more empathic person.

Working with people with ADHD has led me to believe that defensive shifts of attention away from core shame early in life eventually become a generalized habit of mind. It seems that the entire attention apparatus has been undermined so that even when shame is not necessarily a great risk, distraction becomes a habit.

I hope this chapter will inspire you to think more psycho-dynamically about ADHD and begin wondering about the possible role of shame in the symptoms displayed by people with ADHD. I have a strong anti-medication bias, although I believe cognitive behavioral strategies can be extremely helpful. And I have also come to believe that a fully engaged, a joyful therapist is the most helpful intervention when defenses against shame are paramount.

For people who have ADHD, I can only say that only sincerely happy, helping, and joyful partners can help them achieve their goals.

Chapter 18:
Narcissism Versus ADHD

T hrough this book, I hope that the content will help you cope, heal, and better navigate the relationships in all spheres of your life. Now we confront another condition.

Narcissistic Personality Disorder is characterized by arrogant behavior, a lack of empathy for others, and a desire for admiration—all of which must be present at work and in relationships constantly. Narcissistic people are typically characterized as arrogant, self-centered, manipulative, and demanding. In short, narcissists have a strong sense of self-worth. However, narcissism is not synonymous with self-esteem; people with high self-esteem are frequently humble, but narcissists rarely. It was originally assumed that narcissists have strong self-esteem on the outside but are insecure on the inside. However, new evidence suggests that narcissists are secure or grandiose on both levels.

As we all know, ADHD has two components. The two pieces are inattention and hyperactivity/impulsivity. So let's talk about inattention. First, the inattention aspect of attention deficit hyperactivity disorder looks like not being able to pay attention to details, not being able to sustain attention, not listening when spoken to, not being able to follow through on stuff, being very disorganized, and not liking tasks that require sustained attention.

A great example might be reading or being in class, or engaged in a job that requires you to sit down and focus one task for a long time. These people tend to misplace their belongings. They tend to be distractible and forgetful. In many adult presentations, we see more ADD versus ADHD because of age, hyperactivity, and impulsivity. These are the folks who are very fidgety. They have difficulty sitting still in one place for a long time. They talk a lot, they interrupt people, and they have difficulty waiting. But the question is, where does this begin? And where does narcissism end? Interestingly, there is some overlap with narcissistic abuse.

People who are experiencing narcissistic abuse may look and experience themselves as being very inattentive. People who are actively going through narcissistic abuse can be very distractible. They can be very forgetful. And this inattentiveness may not be because they have attention deficit disorder. It may be because of all the ongoing stresses of narcissistic abuse, ruminating about it, not knowing what they are going home to and when the rage will happen again. Then what happens is the person gets called out by a narcissistic partner or narcissistic boss, being gaslighted by them about their distraction.

The reason you are struggling with inattentiveness is that you are constantly in this really unpredictable, chaotic, confusing space, right? It is hard to be attentive as that rumination and confusion takes a toll on your mental resources. The interesting part is to tease out how much of that inattentiveness is actually due to stress. And with the removal of that stress, the capacity to sustain attention would be intact. Now, where it gets really interesting when we talk about narcissism is that a vast number of narcissistic people will say, I just have ADHD. That is an out. When we look at high conflict and personality patterns, there is a high overlap between that personality style and ADHD, particularly impulsivity.

What else do we see in narcissistic people? They do not pay attention to detail because they think, "I cannot be bothered with that? These details are somebody else's problem." By contrast, a person with pure ADHD just does not have the attention to detail. Do you see the difference? A lack of attention to detail may fit more in the ADHD realm along with the inability to pay attention and not listening when spoken to.

Let us say someone is on a phone call and cannot understand what the other person is saying. Somebody who is narcissistic might have attention deficit qualities - distracted and looking at their phone, but not interested in knowing the unheard speech. A person with full-blown ADHD will say, sorry, could you say that again. There will be an empathic awareness that their inability to pay attention is not positive or pleasant for the other person.

Disorganization are distractibility are among the many traits we see in narcissism. They go along with hyperactivity and especially impulsivity.

Such people fidget and talk all the time, sometimes interrupting others. The challenge is that many narcissistic people may not even have been worked up formally for attention deficit disorder. They often use it as a way to excuse her inattention. "I cannot sit here and listen to you talk. I have ADHD." It implies: I have an illness, a legit illness, and cannot be bothered listening.

Meanwhile, they talk excessively for an hour about themselves. The ADHD diagnosis they give themselves is to avoid responsibility or the need to change their behavior.

"I am sorry, I cannot do time management. I have ADHD."

"I am sorry, I cannot do this particular part of the job. I have ADHD."

"I am sorry, I cannot listen to you. I have ADHD".

It is a go-nowhere situation. In narcissism, we have antagonistic symptoms. We do not see them with ADHD as a rule: inattentive symptomatology or impulsive and hyperactive symptomatology. They are entitled, lack empathy, are grandiose and seeking validation. Narcissists have inner rage creating the antagonism. They have no interest in what other people are saying, more from contempt or a lack of empathy.

There is also a condition called conversational narcissism when a person hijacks a conversation. Everything becomes about them. Someone might be talking about their vacation and they will say, "Oh, well, let me tell you about this house," Never does anyone get to speak. And when someone says, "Oh, you are not going to believe this. I rented this cool car for a day", the narcissist will say, "Well, I have owned five of those". They just hijack every conversation.

The other dynamic we see in ADHD with narcissistic symptoms is interrupting a lot. The reason is that they are not listening in the first place. They have what I call contemptuous inattention. Inattention in a person could be fidgeting, having trouble focusing. With the contemptuous version you see facial gestures and a lack of interest, which is invalidating.

Obviously, impulsivity manifests in so many ways such as risky behavior or doing things that can harm other people. Some of you may be wondering how we actually evaluate for ADHD. How do we determine that someone has it? It has largely been a pediatric issue for the longest time, something that happens to kids 18 and under who are jumping out of their desks at school, not being able to pay attention or daydreaming while looking out the window.

However, in the last few decades, we are seeing it much more in adults. In order to diagnose it, the therapist will give the client a checklist. The therapist needs to evaluate the behavior in various settings – as a parent or partner, for example, or even with a client. We get multiple reports about what the patient says and does.

A person undergoes neuropsychological testing, where we very formally and at a much more granular level look at their attentional abilities through a series of tests. A long clinical interview generally lets us know if someone has ADHD. Most therapists assessing for ADHD do not even stop to think about narcissism as well, but you would want to account for both conditions.

Someone with both a narcissistic personality and ADHD often has a contemptuous manifestation of the typical ADHD symptoms. A lot of people out there are narcissistic but have actually never been appropriately assessed for ADHD. Nonetheless, they try to use it to get away with explain their contemptuous disregard for other people.

Some people find that their ADHD causes them a lot of problems in their adult life. In school, it left them feeling insecure as a student. It might have even made them more vulnerable to bullying or falling in with the wrong crowd. there might be some lifelong issues that started young and linger. It may have even resulted in having more problems within the family unit. No doubt their parents were upset because they were a handful. Kids with ADHD have a slightly greater risk in adolescence and middle school to use substances, maybe in an attempt to self-medicate. They tend to engage in risky behaviors; so they will experiment with drugs along with their impulsive peers.

People with ADHD, in my experience, are very "inwardly focused." A lot is going on in their heads, and they spend a lot of time attempting to keep it under control or simply follow the numerous interesting "paths" they find there. This leads them to ignore the needs of those around them because they are so absorbed in themselves. Furthermore, people with ADHD have a decreased capacity to read others' emotional/physical clues. When these factors are combined, non-ADHD partners may feel that their ADHD partner is egotistical when they are persistently distracted. Accusations of a lack of empathy are frequently followed by marital disintegration. It can happen at any time, but generally the ADHD partner may have withdrawn from his or her partner to avoid conflict or they harden their attitude in response to feeling pushed or complained about constantly.

But then, going into adulthood, such people wonder what they can do about it other than taking medication to manage the symptoms. A lot of these adults will say, "without this medication, I really would not get through the day." It is very important as part of their treatment. Sometimes used are structural fixes, having a routine, making sure things are put away or labeled in a careful ways. They learn to engage in daily practices such as mindfulness and chunking tasks into smaller bits instead of sitting down to do something for three hours. One tactic is to set little alarms every 15 to 20 minutes as logical breaks. They can walk around and then get back to matters at hand. It makes a task seem less onerous or overwhelming. But if there is narcissism involved with the presentation of ADHD, structural fixes may not be sufficient because their antagonistic attitude is making things worse.

It can exacerbate a tangled relationship when one person says, I have ADHD. The partner feels that this is not just about them being inattentive. It is a contemptuous, almost reckless disregard for what others have to say. There is a difference.

Chapter 19:
Questions and Answers

Q: What are some of the ways that ADHD symptoms can wreak havoc on a relationship?

A: ADHD symptoms add constant and predictable patterns to marriages. As long as the ADHD goes undiagnosed or undertreated, these patterns can make both partners miserable, lonely, and overwhelmed. They may fight frequently or retreat from each other to defend themselves from harm. The non-ADHD partner's usual response is to become overly bossy and nagging ("The only way to get anything done around here..."). In contrast, the ADHD partner gets increasingly disengaged ("Who wants to be with someone who is constantly angry?").

If ADHD is affecting your relationship, you may notice any of the following patterns:

- Nagging and/or rage regularly.
- The distribution of household tasks is radically asymmetric.
- One spouse is always responsible (a "parent" position), whereas the other is consistently inconsistent or irresponsible (a "child" role)
- Your courtship was fantastic, and you could not get enough of one other; however, one of your partners is no longer paying attention at all.
- You argue all the time, even over trivial matters.
- One partner does not appear to remember agreements well or seems to be tuned out.
- One partner has a difficult time following through on things that have been agreed upon.
- the sexual relationship has ended.

As a result, the divorce and marital dysfunction rates for ADHD-affected couples are nearly double those of ADHD-unaffected couples.

The good news is that knowing the function of ADHD in a relationship can help you save your marriage.

Q: An ADHD spouse in the middle of a marriage crisis: How does it feel?

A: ADHD symptoms fall on a spectrum. Some people have no problems with ADHD in one or more areas of their life, such as their job, but struggle in others, such as relationships. ADHD interferes with almost everything, according to those with the most severe symptoms.

An individual with ADHD who is in a troubled marriage may have the following symptoms, among others:

- Overwhelmed, either secretly or openly, because managing daily life with ADHD requires far more effort than most people realize.
- Subordinate to a spouse who is "in charge," especially if parent/child dynamics are present.
- Feeling unloved because he or she is constantly reminded that he or she needs to "transform" or do better.
- Thinking I am afraid of failing again. As a relationship deteriorates, typical ADHD instability adds to anxiety about what will happen the next time one fails.

  People with ADHD recognize that the world does not work the same way for them as it does for others. Their minds are frequently "racing," "noisy," or "cluttered;" and as a result, they perceive and experience the world in ways that others do not. One young man compared his ADHD brain to "having the Library of Congress in your head without the card catalog."

Q: What about the partner who does not have ADHD? What is useful for the ADHD partner to understand about his or her non-ADHD partner's experiences?

A: The non-ADHD experience, like that of the ADHD spouse, ranges from slightly troublesome to unmanageable. On the milder end of the range is the spouse who is astonished and dissatisfied that her ADHD husband is not paying attention to her. At the extreme end of the spectrum is the partner who feels entirely overburdened by the responsibilities she has taken on because she believes her spouse cannot accomplish them. She dislikes herself and her husband, and she is frequently furious and annoyed by her situation.

The experience of the non-ADHD partner often progresses from happy to bewildered to furious to hopeless. He or she might have the following thoughts:

- She is lonely since her husband is too preoccupied to pay attention to her.
- Angry and emotionally inhibited - anger at the untreated ADHD partner's failure to adjust interactions or follow through on responsibilities can pervade many interactions. In an attempt to control this, a non-ADHD partner may "bottle it up" inside.
- Stressed out - too many obligations, insufficient support, and too much rage can make a non-ADHD partner's relationship poisonous.
- Exhausted, despairing, and depressed as living with someone who does not manage their ADHD can be a great challenge. The recurrent pattern of how untreated ADHD symptoms manifest in the relationship leads to the idea that nothing will ever change.

Q: You discuss the damaging symptom-response-response cycle in your book. Describe what this is, how it can be harmful in a relationship, and how to break this bad habit?

A: It is common to blame ADHD symptoms for all marital troubles, but this is not the case. Both couples have significant roles to play in their marital misery. ADHD symptoms can cause unforeseen, often subtle, strains on a marriage, as well as numerous misunderstandings. However, the devastation is caused by the entire pattern, including the symptoms and the symptoms' response.

A classic example revolves around distraction, one of the most common and significant symptoms of ADHD. A partner with ADHD who is inattentive is generally simply not paying attention to his or her spouse. If the spouse is unaware of ADHD, she would most likely perceive the lack of attention as "he no longer cares about me." As a result, she grows increasingly frustrated with his lack of attention and begins to be short and furious with him. He hears the rage but does not know where it came from, so he feels hurt and angered by it. They are now in a downward, reinforcing spiral.

On the other hand, if the couple is aware of the ADHD, the unnoticed spouse can say, "You have been distracted recently, and I am lonely. Can we go on a date and spend quality time together?" Thus, you can see how recognizing the presence of the ADHD symptom and responding appropriately can have a major influence. But do not get me wrong: the symptom is at the start of the cycle. Thus the symptoms must be managed or worked around if a problematic couple wants to improve their relationship in the long run.

Q: You also tell couples that it is not an issue of "trying harder," but rather of "trying differently." What exactly does this mean?

A: You can use your knowledge about ADHD to select strategies that will help you achieve your goals. These are what I refer to as "ADHD sensitive" techniques. For example, simply trying harder to remember to do a chore in the future is unlikely to help because the symptom "distraction" would interfere, and the task will be forgotten. In contrast, setting the alarm on your phone to remind you to perform the chore at the time it has to be done is likely to work quite well. This is because the ADHD spouse may be distracted in the meantime, but the alarm brings the chore back to the forefront of his or her mind at just the correct time.

Q: What are some critical aspects that couples who are still battling with the "ADHD Effect" in their relationship but are learning more about the occurring patterns should be aware of going ahead, mending, and rebuilding their marriage?

A: This is a two-person project. To succeed, you must both accept responsibility for your own challenges and improvements. On the other hand, you cannot be held accountable for your partner's changes, including whether or not to consider medication for ADHD. Learn everything you can about your differences and your partner's experience. It will increase your empathy, patience, and even motivation. Improve the ADHD treatment. Medication alone will not suffice. I recommend that couples consider a multi-pronged approach to treatment.

Consider how to improve your relationship rather than how to save your marriage. This will keep you focused on what matters most: how the two of you interact with each other rather than the details of your relationship. Most unhappy couples are preoccupied with logistics (who is doing what).

Marriage, in the end, is about joy. As you work through the steps for repairing your relationship, remember to find something to enjoy or laugh about as often as you can. Make time to generate joy, not only to fix things. You both require relief from the work needed to change behaviors that have been formed over time.

Q: What about needing more attention as a non-ADHD spouse? He/she feels overlooked, but it is hard to explain to them that the non-ADHD person needs more attention.

A: For the one who does not have ADHD, it often feels like the world has to revolve around the ADHD spouse because they are the one with more needs. They are the one who needs reminders. They are the ones who have a very hard time focusing on things that do not excite them or something they are passionate about. Trying to get him/her interested is really, really hard, even core things. So what you have to do is not get emotional about it. Do not get upset or angry. You have to tell them, "Hey, this is what I need." Communication is the key.

Conclusion

A Few tips for the non-ADHD partner

Some days, you do not have the energy to deal with your partner's ADHD symptoms. What are your options? Here are nine survival techniques to help you...

Maintain your composure.

Blowing out will intensify your status as a nag or difficult spouse. This is not in your best interests since it allows your partner to dismiss you rather than respect you. So, instead of becoming enraged, let the matter (whatever it was) "slip by" you when you lack the energy to deal with it calmly at the time.

Make a note of it.

Non-ADHD partners are sometimes hesitant to let things go because they are afraid their partner would "drift off," which will be the end of it. To counteract this, make a note of what has to be handled so you can deal with it later, perhaps with the help of a counselor. For example, you could write "late getting kids to school by 30 minutes on Tuesday" or "interrupted numerous times during dinner on Friday." After a while, you may see trends that will assist you in persuading your partner that their behavior is more difficult than they believed.

Be selfish and do something nice for yourself.

When confronted with persistent ADHD symptoms, non-ADHD spouses tend to focus on their ADHD spouse rather than on themselves...to their peril.

In my situation, the more unhappy I became, the more I began to obsess about my husband - what he was not doing and should have been doing, how much his actions affected our family, how insensitive he was, how untrustworthy he was, and so on. I forgot about myself, which was unhealthy! So, when things get rough, do something for yourself - take a nap, finish that project that has been nagging you (unapologetically dump the kids on your spouse), get a massage, read a book in the park, eat some healthy food, go to bed early, or exercise. All of these will help your mental state, especially the last one (exercise). Or, as the advertisement states, "you earned it!"

Demand to be heard...later.

It is not the time to confront complex matters while you are exhausted and frustrated. Instead, wait until you are in a better mood, sit down with your partner and calmly express what you require. Of course, you do not want to give up on your requirements. Still, you also do not want to undermine yourself by appearing unreasonable, furious, or difficult to deal with. (This works against you because it offers your partner a reason to withdraw – and nothing gets addressed that way!)

Maintain a journal.

Sometimes weariness is another way of saying, "I do not have any more ideas." Writing in a journal can help you uncover your emotions and consider alternative solutions to your difficulties. It can also provide much-needed quiet, self-focus time.

Make a new friend.

Take a walk together, go out for dinner or drinks, or visit a local museum. If necessary, get a sitter. Knowing you have somebody who cares about you can help you get through difficult times. Unfortunately, too many non-ADHD couples isolate themselves while attempting to work through marital problems and keep control of their lives and the home.

Listen.

When you have regained the energy to interact again, remember to listen. All too frequently, non-ADHD spouses become accustomed to "ordering" their ADHD spouses around and fail to recognize that they are not truly listening to their partner. Do not order on the other hand. Instead, pay attention and ask questions. This will promote engagement in your partner, which may be sufficient to re-energize you.

Hire someone to do the work if you can.

It is out to take something off your plate. Housework, yard work, filing, decluttering, and organizing, and babysitting are all tasks that can be effectively outsourced. In addition, this form of organization will aid in the prevention of future stress.

Plan.

The eight suggestions above should help you find new energy and approaches. Planning to get out of your current rut will make you feel better.

Tips for the adult ADHD partner

Organizing and Controlling Clutter

ADHD's defining characteristics are inattention and distractibility, making organization one of the most difficult challenges for individuals with the illness. If you have ADHD, the notion of getting organized, whether at work or home, might be overwhelming.

You can, however, learn to break activities down into smaller parts and systematically organize yourself. Implementing various structures and routines and utilizing daily planners and reminders can help you maintain organization and control clutter.

Develop and maintain structure and neat habits.

To organize a room, home, or office, begin by categorizing your belongings and determining which are important and which may be stored or discarded. Then, make a habit of taking notes and making lists to help you stay organized. Regular, everyday routines can help you keep your newly structured structure.

Make some room. Consider what you require daily and discover storage bins or closets for what you do not. Set aside special spaces for items such as keys, money, and other easily misplaced objects. Get rid of anything you do not need.

Make use of a calendar app or a day planner. Using a day planner or calendar on your smartphone or computer effectively might help you recall appointments and deadlines. You can also use electronic calendars to set up automatic reminders so that scheduled occasions do not slip your memory.

Make use of lists. Keep track of frequently planned chores, projects, deadlines, and appointments by using lists and notes. Keep all lists and notes inside your daily planner if you chose to use one. There are also other options for usage on your smartphone or PC. For example, look for to-do applications or task managers.

Deal with it right now. Filing paperwork, clearing up messes, and returning phone calls quickly, rather than later will help you avoid forgetfulness, clutter, and procrastination. If a task can be performed in two minutes or less, do it right away rather than postpone it until later.

Control your paper trail.

If you have ADHD, the paperwork could be a big source of your disorganization. You may, however, put an end to the never-ending mounds of mail and documents strewn around your kitchen, desk, or office. It simply takes a bit of time and effort to put together a paperwork system that works for you.

Daily, deal with mail. Set aside some minutes every day to deal with mail, preferably as soon as you bring it in, ideally as soon as you bring it in. It is helpful to have a designated area where you can go through your mail and decide whether to discard it, file it, or act on it.

Reduce your reliance on paper. Reduce the amount of paper you must deal with instead of paper copies, electronic request statements, and bills. You may reduce junk mail in the United States by opting out of the Direct Marketing Association's (DMA) Mail Preference Service.

Create a file system. Dividers or distinct file folders should be used for different documents (such as medical records, receipts, and income statements). Label and color-code your files to make it easier to find what you are looking for.

Time management and scheduling adhesion.

Time management issues are a common side effect of ADHD. You may constantly lose track of time, missed deadlines, be late, or misjudge the time required for tasks, or perform things in the wrong order. In addition, many adults with ADHD spend so much time on one task (known as "hyper-focusing") It's as if they don't have time to do anything else. These issues can leave you feeling irritated and inadequate, and they also irritate others. There are, however, alternatives to help you better manage your time.

Time management advice

Adults with attention deficit disorder frequently have a distorted perspective of time. So, use the oldest trick in the book: a clock to synchronize your sense of time with everyone else's. Make yourself a clock-watcher. Monitor your time with a wristwatch or use a huge wall or desk clock to keep track of your time. Then, when you begin a task, record the time by stating it aloud or writing it down.

Make use of timers. Set time limits for each task and use a timer or alarm to notify you when your time is up. Consider setting the alarm to go off at regular intervals for longer jobs to keep you productive and conscious of how much time is passing.

Allow yourself more time than you believe you require. Adults with ADHD are famously lousy at calculating how long something will take. So please give yourself a ten-minute buffer for every thirty minutes you estimate it will take you to get somewhere or accomplish a task.

Make plans to arrive early and create reminders. For example, make appointments for fifteen minutes earlier than they are. Set reminders to ensure you leave on time and make sure you have everything you need ahead of time, so you're not rushing for your keys or phone when it's time to leave

Advice on Prioritization

Because persons with ADHD frequently battle with impulse control and move from one subject to another, finishing activities and huge projects can be challenging. To get around this, do the following:

- Determine which tasks should be completed first. Ask yourself what the most critical task is that you need to complete, and then prioritize your other tasks after that.
- Take each step one at a time. Divide major undertakings or jobs into smaller, more achievable steps.
- Maintain your focus. Stick to your schedule and use a timer to enforce it if necessary to avoid becoming sidetracked.

Understand how to say no

Adults with ADHD who are impulsive may accept too many initiatives at work or too many social commitments. On the other hand, a crammed schedule might leave you feeling overwhelmed, overtired and negatively impact the quality of your job. Saying no to some commitments may increase your ability to complete tasks, maintain social obligations, and live a healthy lifestyle. Before agreeing to something new, double-check your schedule.

Money and bill management advice

Money management necessitates budgeting, planning, and organization, which can be difficult for many persons with ADHD. Many conventional money management systems do not function well for persons with ADHD because they necessitate too much time and attention to detail. However, if you create your own simple and consistent method, you may be able to get control of your finances and prevent overspending, late bills, and penalties for missing deadlines.

Keep an eye on your spending

An honest assessment of your financial status is the first step in gaining control of your budget. Begin by keeping note of all expenses, no matter how minor, for a month. You will be able to effectively assess where your money is going as a result of this. For example, The amount of money you wasted on impulse purchases and pointless items may surprise you. This snapshot of your spending habits can then be used to construct a monthly budget based on your income and demands.

Determine how you can stay within your budget. For example, if you spend too much money at restaurants, you can establish an eating-at-home plan that includes time for grocery shopping and meal preparation.

Create basic money management and bill-paying system

Create a simple, orderly system for saving documents, receipts and keeping track of bills. The ability to manage banking on the computer might be a gift that keeps on giving to an adult with ADHD. Online money management means minimal paperwork, no sloppy handwriting, and no forgotten slips.

Change to internet banking. Signing up for internet banking can make the hit-or-miss procedure of budget-balancing a thing of the past. Your online account will maintain track of all deposits and payments, and your balance will be tracked to the penny every day. You may also enable automatic payments for your normal monthly invoices and login if you need to pay unexpected or one-time bills. The best aspect is that there are no misplaced envelopes or late fees.

Configure bill-paying reminders. If you do not want to set up automated payments, you can still make bill paying easier by using electronic reminders. For example, you may be able to set up SMS or email reminders through online banking, or you may be able to plan them through your calendar app.

Use technology to your advantage. You may use free services to keep track of your finances and accounts. They usually take some time to set up, but they update automatically once you have linked your accounts. These types of tools can make your financial life easier.

Put an end to impulse purchases

ADHD impulsivity and shopping can be a deadly combo. It has the potential to put you in debt while also making you feel guilty and embarrassed. However, a few clever approaches can help you avoid impulsive purchases.

- Keep your checkbook or credit cards at home and just use cash to shop.

- Except for one credit card, all of them should be shredded. When you go shopping, make a list of what you want and stick to it.

- When shopping, keep a running total with a calculator (hint: it is on your phone).

- Avoid places where you are likely to overspend, throw away catalogs as they arrive, and block communications from shops.

Workplace Tips for Staying Focused and Productive

A man sitting on the sofa, coffee cup in one hand, smiling as he looks down at laptop display, brick and white-painted walls behind ADHD can offer unique workplace issues. The things you may find most difficult—organization, task completion, sitting still, and listening quietly—are the very things you are frequently asked to perform all day.

It is not simple to balance ADHD and a demanding career, but by personalizing your employment environment, you may capitalize on your strengths while reducing the negative impact of your ADHD symptoms.

Get your workplace organized

Organize your office, cubicle, or desk by taking small, doable steps. Then, to maintain tidy and organized, employ the following strategies:

- Set aside time each day for the organization because a messy desk always created distractions. Set aside 5 to 10 minutes each day to clear your desk and organize your files. Experiment with storing items inside your desk or bins to not become an unnecessary distraction in your workspace.
- Make use of colors and lists. Color-coding can be quite beneficial to those with ADHD. Managing forgetting can be accomplished by writing everything down.
- Prioritize. More critical chores should be prioritized on your to-do list so that you remember to do them first. Establish timelines for everything, even if they are self-imposed.

Put an end to distractions

When you have attention challenges, where you work, and what is around you can have a big impact on how much you can get done. Inform your coworkers that you need to concentrate and use the following tactics to reduce distractions:

- It is important where you work. Consider moving your office to an adjacent building or conference room. If you're attending a lecture or a conference, try to sit nearer the speaker and away from people who talk during the session.
- Reduce external commotion. Maintain a clutter-free workspace by orienting your workstation toward a wall. "Do Not Disturb" signs may also be used to prevent disruptions. For example, allow voicemail to pick up your phone calls and return them later if possible, disable email and social media during particular periods of the day, or even log off the Internet entirely. Consider noise-canceling headphones or a sound machine if noise distracts you.
- Big ideas should be saved until later. All those wonderful ideas or strange thoughts that keep bursting into your head and distracting you, make a note of them on paper or your smartphone for future reference. Some persons with ADHD like to set aside time to look over all of their notes at the end of the day.

Extend your attention span

As an adult with ADHD, you can focus; it is just that you may struggle to maintain that focus, especially if the activity is not extremely fascinating. For example, boring meetings or lectures are difficult for anyone, but they may be especially difficult for people with ADHD. Persons with ADHD may also have trouble comprehending directions. To increase your focus and ability to follow directions, try the following suggestions:

- Make a written record of it. If you are attending a meeting, lecture, workshop, or another gathering that requires your full concentration, request a copy of the essential materials ahead of time, such as a meeting agenda or lecture outline. Use the written notes to help your active listening and note-taking during the meeting. Writing while listening will assist you in focusing on the speaker's words.

- Directions should be repeated. When someone gives you verbal instructions, repeat them aloud to ensure you understand them.
- Change your position. Move around—at the proper moments and in the right places—to avoid uneasiness and fidgeting. When you're in a meeting, try squeezing a stress ball, as long as you are not disrupting others. Taking a walk or even leaping up and down during a meeting break can also help you focus later.

Suggestions for reducing stress and improving mood

You may suffer from unpredictable sleep, an unhealthy diet, or the effects of too little exercise due to the impulsivity and disorganization that typically accompany ADHD—all of which can lead to extra stress, unpleasant moods, and a sense of being out of control. The most effective strategy to break this pattern is to control your lifestyle habits and establish healthy new routines.

Eating healthy food, lots of sleep, and regular exercising could help you stay calm, limit mood changes, and manage anxiety and depression symptoms. Healthier behaviors can also help minimize ADHD symptoms such as inattention, hyperactivity, and distractibility, while routines can make your life feel more manageable.

Exercising and spending time outside

Working out is maybe the most positive and efficient technique to improve ADHD hyperactivity and inattention. Exercising can reduce stress, boost your mood, relax your thoughts, and work off excess energy and anger that can interfere with relationships and feeling stable.

Every day, you should exercise. Choose something active and enjoyable to commit to, such as a team sport or working out with a friend. Exercising outside can help with stress release because persons with ADHD often benefit from sunlight and greenery. Try soothing exercises like mindful walking, yoga, or tai chi. They can educate you to control your attention and impulses better, in addition to easing tension.

Get lots of rest

Lack of sleep might worsen symptoms of adult ADHD, lowering your ability to manage stress and keep focus during the day. However, simple modifications to one's daily activities can go a long way toward ensuring a good night's sleep.

- Avoiding caffeine in the late afternoon is recommended.

- Exercise aggressively and regularly, but not within an hour of going to bed.

- Create a consistent and calm "bedtime" regimen that includes a hot shower or bath right before bed.

- Maintain a consistent sleep-wake routine, including on weekends.

Consume healthy food

While poor eating habits may not cause ADHD, they might exacerbate symptoms. However, simple modifications in what and how you consume can significantly decrease distractibility, hyperactivity, and stress levels.

- Consume modest meals throughout the day.

- Sugar and junk food should be avoided as much as possible.

- Make healthy protein a part of every meal.

- Every day, aim for multiple servings of fiber-rich whole grains.

Mindfulness

Regular mindfulness meditation can help you fight distractions, reduce impulsivity, increase your focus, and have more control over your emotions, in addition to reducing stress. Because hyperactive symptoms can make meditation difficult for some adults with ADHD, beginning gradually can assist the process. Meditate for brief periods and progressively extend your meditation time as you become more familiar with the technique and improve your ability to focus. The goal is to apply these mindfulness practices in your daily life to stay on track. Experiment with free or low-cost smartphone apps or guided meditations available online.

Tips for Marital Success: For Both of You

Let me share some of the recommendations by my clients and people with ADHD with you. rather for both of you

Concentrate on Treatment

A good ADHD relationship requires accurate ADHD diagnosis and treatment.

"I have diagnosed nine months ago and began treatment, which has significantly impacted me and the way I see our relationship. However, we had 16 years of harm before this. Therefore, my greatest advice is to get medical attention as soon as possible!"

Conquer by division

"In our household, we debate the division of labor," wrote one respondent. *"Asking someone with ADHD to perform all of the housework creates animosity. So my partner does the tasks that I find tedious."*

Discover more about ADHD

Understanding ADHD is essential for understanding one another. It is critical that both spouses, not only the partner with ADHD, know about the condition. In these "mixed" marriages, knowledge equals power. Some people refer to ADHD as the "third partner" in their marriage, and they believe it needs to be respected for the role it performs.

Sincerity in communication

Conversations in ADHD couples rapidly devolve into disputes and upset feelings, so it makes sense to focus on communication skills together. This may necessitate the assistance of a counselor or an online course, but the investment will pay off handsomely for the pair.

Maintain Balance

According to one respondent, a healthy ADHD marriage takes both give and take.

"No one is flawless, including persons who do not have ADHD. However, I never use my ADHD as an excuse for inappropriate behavior. You must accept responsibility without blame or shame."

Accept what you cannot change and change what you can

The ADHD couples we spoke with had made significant strides toward making their relationships work. But they all have to cope with it daily. What distinguishes them is that they and their spouses/partners play with the cards dealt to them. They change what they can and have the serenity to accept what they cannot in 12-step parlance. When both spouses accept ADHD, the likelihood of a strong relationship increases.

The story of Rachel

Rachel has been married to her spouse for 20 years. Ten months ago, she was diagnosed with ADHD. "In the past, he would stand there watching me fold towels. I felt scolded, like if I was not doing it correctly," she explained. "After I got my diagnosis, I told him I did not want to fold towels as he does!"

Rachel has learned to ask for assistance. "I wanted to do everything on my own," she explained. "Now my spouse says, 'You can ask me to do these things, such as vacuuming the cat hair.' It is made my life a lot easier."

"Even with ADHD medication, I sometimes get sidetracked, but I have a better knowledge of the disorder. So, when I stop him in the middle of a sentence, I understand I am doing it and accept responsibility," she explained. "I will say, 'Yes, I did interrupt you, and it was my fault.' Please continue stating what you were saying.'"

According to Rachel, the best part about ADHD in her relationship is her ability to perceive their potential as a couple. "I always surprise him," she added.

"I know now that he does not see the world in the same way that I do. But I like ADHD because it makes me a badass. We have a fantastic relationship today, better than ever!"

www.ingramcontent.com/pod-product-compliance
Lightning Source LLC
Chambersburg PA
CBHW060319030426
42336CB00011B/1126